ADVANCE PRAISE FOR *YOUR SIXTH SENSE*:

"Centuries of writings by visionary Christian, Jewish, Middle Eastern, and Far Eastern mystics reveal that each generation perceives not only many important truths, but also strives to describe the many ways of realizing those truths. In *Your Sixth Sense*, Belleruth Naparstek synthesizes, in a down-to-earth way, the what and how of inner knowing. Gleaned from her interviews with many persons immersed in intuitive ways of seeing and sensing, Naparstek offers instruction so that readers may develop and apply the unusual sensitivities of intuition to their own lives."

> —*Clarissa Pinkola Estés, Jungian psychoanalyst*

"I have personally experienced what has been written. I believe we are entering a period when science will have to confront and study human potential. I suggest skeptics and all those interested in enhancing their psychic potential read this book."

> —*Bernie Siegel, M.D., author of* Love, Medicine
> & Miracles

"Psychic abilities are our birthright, part of who we are. They are also a razor's edge, as every spiritual tradition has realized. Wise guides are needed in exploring this area. Belleruth Naparstek is such a guide. This is a fine contributuion to exploring our human potential."

> —*Larry Dossey, M.D., author of* Prayer Is Good
> Medicine, Healing Words, *and* Recovering the Soul.

"Intuition is not only the sixth sense, it is the most important of all of our senses, integrating the other five with that indefinable but critical 'knowing.' All inventions, science, music, art, and creativity are the proof of intuition. This book is worth reading not only for its rich scientific documentation, but for the twenty-four guidelines to developing your own intuitive ability."

—*C. Norman Shealy, M.D., Ph.D., founding president, American Holistic Medical Association*

"One of the most brilliant books on the subject. A guided tour of psychic ability—what it is, where it comes from, and how it works. Written with eloquence and humor, this work is destined to become 'book of the year.'"

—*Ruth Buczynski, Ph.D., president of the National Institute for the Clinical Application of Behavioral Medicine*

YOUR SIXTH SENSE

Also by Belleruth Naparstek

Staying Well with Guided Imagery

Your Sixth Sense

Activating Your Psychic Potential

BELLERUTH NAPARSTEK

HarperSanFrancisco
An Imprint of HarperCollins*Publishers*

HarperCollins Web Site: http://www.harpercollins.com

HarperCollins®, 📖 ®, and HarperSanFrancisco™ are trademarks of HarperCollins Publishers Inc.

FIRST EDITION

Library of Congress Cataloging-in-Publication Data
Naparstek, Belleruth.
Your sixth sense: activating your psychic potential / Belleruth Naparstek.—1st ed. Includes bibliographical references.
ISBN 0–06–251359–1 (cloth)
ISBN 0–06–251360–5 (pbk.)
1. Psychic ability. 2. Psychics. I. Title.
BF 1031;N35 1997 133.8–DC20 96–30248

97 98 99 00 01 ❖ RRDH 10 9 8 7 6 5

The preparation of the heart is the work
    of humankind;
But the gift of speech comes from the Lord.

Proverbs 16:1

Contents

Acknowledgments   xi
Preface   xiii
Introduction   1

PART ONE
What Psychic Ability Is, How It Works,
Who's Got It and Why

1 Clarifying Some Terms   15
2 How People Come to Be Psychic   27
3 Setting the Stage   51
4 Letting It Happen   75
5 Explaining It: The Physics of ESP, Love, and Imagery   93

PART TWO
Activating and Using Your Psychic Ability

6 Imagery to Access Psi   113
7 Specific Things You Can Do to Cultivate
  and Maintain Psi   153
8 Some General Cautions and Ethical Concerns   179

Appendix A: Brief Bios of the Intuitives   191
Appendix B: The Questionnaire   201
Appendix C: Code of Ethics of the Academy
        of Psychic Arts and Sciences   205

Notes   207
Resources   223

Acknowledgments

I know how lucky I am to have experienced the extraordinary midwifery of my editor, Caroline Pincus, in birthing this baby. I thank her for her extraordinary knowledge of the material, her surgical editorial expertise, and of course her enthusiasm, responsiveness, availability, and honesty. (Honesty is priceless, because, as with my dear friend and agent, Loretta Barrett, when praise finally comes, it can be trusted.)

I also thank my publisher and "discoverer," Tom Grady, who got right away what I was trying to do—better than I did, as it turns out—and wholeheartedly supported this project even in its most unformed, embryonic stages.

I thank Anne Harris, Girl Wonder, for her hard work, dedication, know-how, and feisty leadership in keeping my imagery alive. She picked up the baton and ran with it, farther and faster than anyone thought possible, at a time when nobody else, myself included, wanted to be bothered.

Gobs of gratitude go, as always, to George R. Klein for his generosity, creativity, resourcefulness, and willingness to hang in there with me on our wacky guided imagery audiotape adventure for six bumpy, exciting years.

I thank my whole wonderful support system of precious, magical friends. You know who you are and how much you've sustained me. Thank you, from the bottom of my heart, for your kindness, wisdom, patience, and love.

I also thank my kids, Aaron, Keila, and Abram, who, in spite of compelling, young adult agendas of their own, always managed to be such a supportive, resourceful, encouraging, and proud cheering section. They get that from their dad.

And finally, I thank the remarkable intuitives who helped me write this book—the forty-three extraordinary people I interviewed—a most beautiful collection of human beings, inspiring, generous, and kind. Thank you for showing me that, in spite of indications to the contrary, there really is considerable reason for hope: angels are everywhere.

Preface

I'm a psychotherapist, but this is not a book about psychotherapy, even though I use a lot of examples from my practice to illustrate what I have to say. That's only because therapy is how I spend a lot of my time, and it's what I know best.

This is a book about how to recognize, cultivate, and direct the natural gift that we all are born with: our sixth sense. When all is said and done, our ability to know things in a way that leaps over "normal" cognition and perception and just shows up as a sudden intuition or a pop of psychic awareness is an altogether logical, natural, and predictable human skill. This book shows you how the sixth sense is simply standard-issue equipment, along with our eyes, ears, tongues, noses, and skin. It is only as magical and as ordinary as they are—which is plenty magical enough—but no more and no less.

For instance, years ago, when a client I'd been seeing—an attractive young woman with all the usual struggles—walked into my psychotherapy office, sat down, and started to talk, my throat began to ache. A few moments later, she told me that her grandmother had died over the weekend and that she'd been needing to cry but hadn't yet been able to do so. As a result, she'd been walking around for several days with an uncomfortable lump in her throat. As she began to cry, my throat relaxed and softened back to normal. Later I would wonder, how did *her* lump get into *my* throat? What exactly was going on here?

I can remember another time when a different client, this time a young man, on his way out the door turned back to me and opened his mouth to ask me something. Very naturally and seamlessly I answered, "I promise, I'll have them for you next week." He nodded and left. Sometime later it occurred to me that the question about when I would be able to return his completed insurance forms had never been asked out loud and that neither one of us had noticed.

Nowadays, I take psychic experiences—times of direct knowing and sensing that seem to bypass logic and perception—for granted. I suppose at some point they began to happen so frequently that I stopped noticing them. But in writing this book, I've again started tracking and scrutinizing these events, which not only has turned out to be great fun but also has become something of an eye opener: what has become very clear to me is that this process is going on *all the time.* There's a continuous flow of extrasensory information in each and every one of my sessions, all day long. It makes the work much easier for me and my clients. Quicker, too.

Just last week, for instance, a woman called me for some help in creating some personal imagery to help her with her cancer. I had never spoken with her before—she was referred to me by an out-of-state physician—and she wanted a consultation by telephone. She told me she felt something was missing in the imagery she'd devised for battling multiple myeloma, but she wasn't sure what it was. I asked her to describe what she'd been doing, and she told me she was using the image of polar bears because she felt very drawn to them and saw them as a kind of a personal totem.

As she started describing her imagery of big, gentle polar bears surrounding and looking after her, and of being gently held in a soft, white, furry bear's lap, I began seeing in my own mind's eye the very clear image of a great big *guy* bear, standing upright, forelegs crossed over his chest, looking very powerful, aggressively protective, and very male—in other words, a huge Daddy Bear. He showed up in my mind's eye in the first few minutes of our conversation and just kept on reappearing.

I've learned to trust images that persist in this way, so at one point I asked her if she'd ever thought about including a powerful, protective male bear in her scenario, one that would ensure the safety of all those loving, maternal bears. After all, sometimes some serious butt kicking is necessary for survival, too, not just tender loving care.

Her whole tone changed, and she became very energized, excited, and intrigued. She told me that yes, she supposed she would *love* to have a big, protective male bear looking out for her, but it had never occurred to her to evoke such an image because the males in her life had always been so destructive and unreliable. But perhaps, she said, it was time to invent a trustworthy Daddy Bear for her to count on and incorporate into her imagery.

This led us to an important discussion of her need for more balance in her life, especially between the fiercer, more aggressive aspects of her own personality, which had been pretty well submerged, and her softer, more yielding side, which had all but taken over. (Interestingly enough, multiple myeloma is characterized by an imbalance in the blood, a preponderance of certain kinds of cells and a deficiency of others.) Clearly the Daddy Bear represented a central issue for this woman, and his appearance allowed us to get to it very quickly and easily.[1]

Although I'm pretty certain we would have gotten around to this discussion sooner or later, it wouldn't have happened so quickly. This particular "pop" saved us the time and cost of another session.

Incidents like these happen in psychotherapy all the time. There is something about the warmth and openness, the deep, rich emotional connection in a good counseling relationship, that fosters these psychic pops and intuitive knowings. It's nothing special, really. It's just that these relationships promote a kind of attention and caring that is more focused and concentrated than what we find in most of our day-to-day contacts with people. But in the end, what happens in my office can happen anywhere to anyone, and it often does so in a random kind of way.

But intuitive knowing can be made to happen much more consistently with a little intelligent scrutiny and effort and with certain kinds of practices. So let me describe to you my experience in my therapist's chair, the inner process that over time became so much a part of me and resulted in this continuous influx of intuitive information—what the parapsychology researchers like to call *psi*. Later on in this book, I'll be examining this internal process very closely, teasing out the essential elements of it, comparing it to how other intuitives experience it, and then replicating the process with simple guided imagery exercises for you to follow.

But first let me explain that I've been a psychotherapist for nearly thirty years, and I really love my work—can't imagine not doing it. To this day, nothing gets my attention so completely as people telling me the truth about themselves, and I relish my job of providing a good, safe space where they can do that. I've seen, time and again, that when people can speak about themselves from their hearts, without self-criticism or blame, they can change. My job is pretty simple, really.

Because my attention gets so captivated by this process, over the years I've come to develop a kind of intense focus in my work as I sit in my chair and listen to my clients telling me about their lives. It has become a sort of meditation for me, a state of near-total absorption.

For instance, as my attention becomes caught up in the person sitting across from me, my mind automatically clears itself of whatever was preoccupying it just a few moments earlier. I experience that person with a kind of freshness and curiosity. My usual judgments are put on hold, and my normally urgent sense of time somehow drops away. I become calm and patient. (This is pretty remarkable, really, because, I promise you, I can be a very impatient person when I'm out in the world.)

But even though I'm very relaxed, I'm also very alert. I pick up subtleties, hear unsaid sentences, feel unexpressed feelings, and even see images of the people and places that are being described. (Often, when a client later brings in a photo of someone we've talked about, I'll recognize the person from these in-session images.) I might focus on the colors that pulse around the heads and shoulders of the client. A few years into my practice, I began to see "lights" around my clients—whitish auras that were like soft, bright halos—and then, over time, they evolved into colors of varying intensity, especially pinks, greens, blues, violets, and yellows. These days, I'll sometimes find myself captivated by these colorful, glowing energies, easily perceptible around the client against the backdrop of my white office walls.

And I'm so empathically attuned to my clients when I'm in this state, seeing what they see and feeling what they feel, that I'm aware of an overall, generalized feeling of what I can only describe as *love* for them. I'm so suffused with it, I am easily moved by what they say or do. (This doesn't mean I'm not thinking clearly; on the contrary, my thinking is clearer than usual. But at the same time, I am deeply touched by them in this generalized way.) And, where elsewhere in my life I might be critical of their behavior or find fault with their attitudes, in this state compassion crowds out judgment. This doesn't take effort—if it did, I'm sure I'd feel virtuous about it—it just happens.

And most of all, I feel very alive—very present and deeply grateful to be doing this work that I do. A quiet elation fills me as I sit at what has somehow become a glorious kind of meditation for me.

As I said, even though elsewhere in my life I can be stressed, impatient, judgmental, and irritable—the typical reactions, I suppose, of someone always looking to cram yet one more thing into an overfull, Type-A day—I enter this state of mind automatically and without effort just about every time I sit down with one of my clients. Somehow, when I enter the privileged space of these special relationships, I have all the patience of a Buddha.

Now let me be clear that when I talk about focusing on my clients, I'm not talking only about listening to the content of what they have to say or about attending to their thought patterns, feelings, body language, verbal language, and overriding sense of self, or about how all these things fuel whatever difficulties they are having.

Of course, I do that, too. Left-brain business continues as usual, and a separate part of my therapist's mind is on the job, analyzing and computing, juxtaposing feelings with behavior, looking for distortions and self-deception, creating and eliminating categories, comparing this client with others, testing out hypotheses and setting them aside. But this left-brained, analytic process is not what I'm talking about here.

I'm talking about opening my *heart* to this other person, being fully present to them (even while all this analysis is going on in the computerish, left side of my brain) and getting a full *sense* of them. I experience what it's like to be them with all of my senses, with all of my feelings, and in every part of my body. This, more than anything else, is what holds and nurtures the relationship, provides the wherewithal for deep insights in a timely way, and energizes the possibility of change.

In short, I cultivate empathy and compassion—not a bad way to spend the day. And any good therapist worth her aching neck and shoulders will tell you that after the first few years of practice, once enough technical skill has been learned to master the basics, this is how the job gets done.

And this, for the most part, is how I believe my psi ability developed. It slowly and incrementally grew alongside this attitude of openheartedness that unfolded over the years; it developed in a state of mind that suspended time; it showed up with the deep attentional focus of the meditative state. Sometimes information would come to me at times when I wanted to help someone, and my awareness that I didn't know what to do became like a prayer; it seemed that when I surrendered to my helplessness, the right ideas and words would come. And sometimes, simply being bathed in loving feelings, awash in the energy of the open heart, I'd just seem to get lucky and wisdom would show up, like a bright penny on the sidewalk.

In the pages that follow, I talk about the different factors that create the conditions for psychic ability—mine and others'. I'll be looking very carefully at my own process, at what scientific research can tell us about it, at how theoretical physics explains it, and at the experiences of several gifted intuitives whom I've managed to track down and interview at length— over forty people altogether. These varied approaches offer you a comprehensive and balanced look at what this phenomenon is and how and why it works. That's part 1 of this book—what psychic ability consists of, where it comes from, and how it works. Ambitious, I know.

Part 2 is the "how to" part, where I've taken everything that I've learned and incorporated it into specific suggestions and guided imagery exercises that are carefully designed to replicate these psi-generating experiences. I've tested them with lots of people, and I know that they work—sometimes immediately and sometimes incrementally over time.

I say this with some confidence, since I have introduced guided imagery in various workshops and training sessions to all kinds of participants, ranging from the intuitively gifted to those whose third eye seemed virtually cemented shut. Sooner or later, almost everyone was able to make good use of these techniques. Many were astonished by what could happen and what they were able to do; they experienced things they had previously thought impossible. The process created a powerful shift in their view of the world and mobilized profound changes in their ideas about who they actually were.

Guided imagery is, I must tell you, a near-perfect vehicle for psychic development. It's a kind of deliberate, directed daydreaming, a purposeful use of the imagination that automatically alters our consciousness as we use it and drops us down into the clear, receptive state that is so necessary for picking up subtle, intuitive signals at will.

You could say that guided imagery is a specific kind of meditation that causes deep shifts in body, psyche, and spirit (none of which is really separate from the others). Guided imagery presents us with multiple layers of encoded messages, packaged in such a way that the mind and body can wholeheartedly go for them. The images act like depth charges that reverberate somewhere beneath the surface, over and over again.

If designed artfully enough, imagery can capture complex ideas with just a simple phrase or symbol. And when it is constructed knowledgeably, with enough attention to the technical detail necessary to make it work right, imagery is a powerful and effective instrument indeed.

More specifically, guided imagery that opens the heart cuts right to the chase. It's particularly effective at expanding our boundaries, heightening our consciousness, and amplifying the human energy field. This allows us access to enormous amounts of psi data.

Heart-opening imagery is fast, efficient, and effective. Over time, we need less and less of it to gain access to the information available to us. Eventually, the process becomes seamless; we want the information, and, without missing a beat, we get it.

Along with the imagery exercises, the second half of this book also includes a summary of general suggestions for you to follow. Some of what I recommend you've probably heard before—

I know I have—but some you probably haven't. Some of the ideas in this book never crossed my mind until I started having amazing conversations with all sorts of generous, gifted intuitives across the country. I hope I've done justice to their remarkable voices on these pages. Because of them, I'm not the same person who started this book nearly a year ago.

Introduction

Although psychic ability has been variously mystified, glorified, obfuscated, demonized, and reviled, when all is said and done it's nothing more than a basic human capacity, a skill of great practical value, that can be further developed by just about anyone. It's nothing special, except in the way that we are all special. Or let me put it this way: psychic ability is pretty amazing, but *you don't have to be special or extraordinary in any way to use it.* Intuition, ESP, psi, paranormal intelligence, high sense perception, the third eye, the sixth chakra—whatever you choose to call it—is part of our natural human endowment. It's all right there in our genetic hardwiring; it is ours for the asking.

Undoubtedly, some people are born better wired for it, so to speak, than others. But this is no different from the way that some people are born with more athletic ability or musical talent than the norm. Although we may not all be Mickey Mantle or Van Cliburn, we can still play the piano for our enjoyment or throw a ball well enough to play the game.

One thing is certain: whatever skill level you are currently starting with, you can expand it considerably. In fact, I've seen students who appeared to have very little promise in this regard become extremely adept with a simple application of time, effort, and commitment. I confess I was surprised at how skilled they became. And believe me, if some of these folks can do it, you can, too.

If you think about it, you probably can point to times when you've "read" the minds of others, had a gut feeling that overrode logic, or knew what was going to happen before it actually did. Sometimes you knew who was calling before you picked up the phone, or you heard from someone you'd only just thought of that day, after a hiatus of months or even years. And perhaps, too, you've known the feeling of being possessed by a kind of inspiration that had you speaking, writing, or expressing yourself in ways you'd never thought to do consciously. Later, you might look at what you wrote, said, or performed, and think, "Wow, who did *that?* I'd like to meet her."

Because these occurrences seem to arrive unbidden and don't fit into our rationalist view of the world, we usually discount them or forget about them. But we're missing a big opportunity. Because with or without our conscious agreement, just below the surface of our lives, this boundless, abiding intelligence quietly sits and waits for us to recognize it. In all likelihood, it's looking forward to the time when it will be relied upon more, the day when it will achieve some sort of consistent, gainful, above-board employment and finally get the respectability it deserves. I suspect that time is just around the corner.

Certainly I'm aware of the fact that this field of endeavor has gotten no help whatsoever from the tacky stereotypes surrounding it. We are all familiar with them: the sleazy sideshow palm reader with the cheesy costume and the beaded curtain or the flaky New Age flower child who barely has enough sense to come in out of the cold or the demonic cult leader looking to control our minds and exploit our checkbooks.

Of course the "psychic hot lines" beckoning us on television, selling facile predictions of romance, wealth, and whatever else we want to hear to the tune of three dollars a minute, don't enhance the credibility of psi. And channelers with bizarre accents and exotic names, who get to say anything they want but don't have to be accountable for it because it's not *them* talking but some "entity" inhabiting their corpus instead, don't exactly move us to a state of trustfulness, either. (Actually, this tactic reminds me of my oldest son, Aaron, when he was three. When caught doing something wrong, he'd protest with great sincerity, "The *other* Aaron did it!" This little stratagem may be okay for a three-year-old, but it loses its charm when coming from the mouth of a grown-up.)

So let me be clear that this book is designed to help you gain access to your own psychic and intuitive ability in an integrated, practical fashion so that it will better serve you and the people around you. You'll be able to measure the value of the information you get by the effect it has on the people and projects around you and, not least of all, on yourself.

You won't need to get advice from somebody in a costume, because you'll see that you already have access to all the information you need. And you'll be able to get at it more and more readily with the benefit of consistent practice and experience. It won't make you any more special or extraordinary than you already are, which is plenty special enough. And you'll remain responsible for what you say and do, because you won't be leaving your body to make room for some wise old spirit with an exotic name who can hold sway with *your* mouth. This will be *you* thinking and talking, in a fully integrated way, part of your everyday, normal, grounded experience of living.

And you'll experience some intriguing side benefits. Even if you're a pretty terrific person to start with, engaging in this process might make an even better human being of you, because it will ask you to open your heart in order to gain access to psi. This is what's been happening in my psychotherapist's chair all these years. Very simply put, when the heart is opened to its own boundless, compassionate, loving energy, boundaries dissolve and intuitive information starts showing up.

And the guided imagery process as I've designed it is even good for your health. The heart-opening imagery that generates feelings of love, compassion, and gratitude will also speed up healing from cuts, fractures, and burns; it will lower blood pressure, blood sugar, and blood cholesterol levels; and it will even elevate the count of certain powerful immune cells in the blood. Imagery has long been acknowledged to be an effective reducer of anxiety and depression because it has a direct impact on neurohormone levels in the body. Researchers like Jeanne Achterberg, Howard Hall, Frank Lawlis, Karen Olness, and Nicholas Hall all have found that imagery produces effects indicating heightened immune functioning: increases in neutrophil activity, the presence of thymosin-alpha-1 hormone in the blood, and immunoglobulin A in the saliva.[1]

In fact, it was in this context of health that I first realized how potent a technique imagery could be for delivering up psychic information. People who were using my imagery audiotapes for cancer, diabetes, and arthritis reported getting intuitive insights and psychic pops as they listened to the tapes. They weren't looking to have this happen—it just did. These gratuitous visits of insight struck me as particularly compelling evidence that guided imagery was indeed a fertile breeding ground for psi.

Aside from the fact that heart-opening imagery is extremely good for your health, I favor it for another reason as well. The heart route is a good, safe way to travel. It's reliable. It works for most people. And it's gentle and kind. So even though many other technologies and systems will crank open your third eye, this, to my way of thinking, is the method of choice.

Unfortunately, we've heard a little too much about people "becoming psychic" from experiences of terror, trauma, or abuse in their past or from having had a near-death experience

(NDE) or some sort of out-of-body experience (OBE). And yes, it's true that people's psi skills can get activated in these ways. Perhaps, because these avenues are dramatic, they've gotten an inordinate amount of attention and are mistakenly perceived as the primary way to open the third eye. But the open-heart route is a far easier, more pleasant, and more commonplace way to expand psychically; the third eye does not necessarily have to be bonked open by some horrendous event.

This gentle, gradual heart route is reliable, satisfying, and effective. When we are relaxed and can genuinely welcome the emotions of love, empathy, compassion, and gratitude, the closed lid over the slumbering third eye gets a little tap. When we begin to consistently connect with others from this rich and tender, openhearted place, that eyelid starts to stir, even flutter a bit.

And when we have so cultivated this openhearted place and so expanded the energy around our hearts that our boundaries have stretched to include others, then that eye really starts to open. When, from a place of strength and well-being, we allow our normally limited sense of self to dissolve, we can take in the whole world and every intelligent, vibrating particle in it. The whole universe can fit easily into the vast, boundless space of the open heart. And there's room to spare for several worlds more.

And from the open heart, we get the true picture of exactly who and what we are. The view is stunning. We become an enormous energy field that has instantaneous reach everywhere. When this happens, the third eye has popped wide open. And we can consciously keep it open for long stretches at a time by continually reinvoking this openhearted state.

And, just as important, we can consciously close it, too, when we miss the grounded feel of our identities and skins and when our psyches could use a little shut-eye. At some point that's unique for each of us, the process of opening and closing our psychic perception starts to function automatically. Then we can routinely process psychic information along with all of our other everyday thoughts and perceptions. The process becomes integrated and seamless.

This is why so many psychotherapists and health care professionals—particularly the softies who have big hearts to begin with—become so psychically attuned over their years of practice, once they've gained enough technical mastery to relax into their work and feel their genuine love for their clients. This is also why so many mothers are telepathically connected to their children and intuitively know, even at a distance, when they are in trouble. It's why a young woman in Boston knows the exact moment that a beloved grandparent in Chicago has died.

This, too, is why people in that first high, hormonal rush of romantic love, when they are wild about everyone and everything, report so many synchronicities and psychic "hits" to their long-suffering, eye-rolling friends. And this is why research labs that study these phenomena (which they prefer to call "psi") are known to report stronger findings when the lab environment is perceived as warm, supportive, and caring.[2]

Aside from the fact that this heart-opening route to psychic development has been part of my own experience and suits me personally, I have another reason for preferring this way of gaining access to psi. Working with the open heart has certain built-in safeguards. There is no cruelty in the vast, rich territory of the heart, no need for power or ascendancy over others. In fact, in most Eastern systems of thought the heart, or fourth chakra, is the meeting ground of spirit and flesh, heaven and earth, and therefore the doorway to enlightenment. It is where our cruder energies are transformed into love and compassionate wisdom. It is a place of great nourishment, empathy, and kindness. So the open heart is a good place to cultivate and inhabit, in and of itself; all of us could use more time in its generous spaces, with or without the intention of psychic opening.

And aside from the practical value of opening up our psychic ability—it warns us of danger, fuels much of our creative work, helps us make inspired choices, and gives us insights into ourselves and others—it has an overriding spiritual contribution to make at this time in human history.

I think—and I'm certainly not the first person to say this—that we've entered a new stage of our human evolution, a time when the development of our psychic capacity is essential to our survival. Without a new and stronger kind of psychic attunement, without a deeper sense of spiritual connectedness to the whole, and without a much larger sense of self than we as a species have ever attained, our planet could easily die from out-of-control aggression, territoriality, and greed.

So it's no coincidence that we find ourselves in a time of great interest in psychic phenomena, of widespread longing for connection to our spiritual core. More and more people are looking for ways to join with the mysterious, the wider perspective, the divine, the world of spirit. Cultivating our psychic ability through the open heart is a universal and direct way to do this, one that transcends the boundaries of specific religions, philosophies, and nationalities.

ψ ψ ψ

In the pages that follow, I'll offer you what I hope is a comprehensive, balanced, and detailed look at the process of developing your native intuitive ability. I'll look at this from several vantage points. First, I'll explain how I came to develop my own intuitive skills—through my work as a psychotherapist and through my personal life experiences.

I'll also examine what parapsychological research has taught us about "psi-conducive" conditions. Although more such research should be available than currently is, we still have enough to work with.

And, using data from my interviews with forty-three highly skilled intuitives—people who shared with me the details of their own development and inner process—I'll look at the ways they developed their precognitive, telepathic, and healing abilities and at the different life events and daily practices that they credit for their growth and development. I'll take a very careful, magnified look at their process *in the moment,* using the instants just before and during the time of receiving information in order to replicate the common elements in my imagery.

I found my sample of intuitives through professional networking, word of mouth, and repeated recommendations. I screened all my informants and eliminated the few who struck me as too confused, unskilled, or ethically iffy.

Initially, I worried about getting a balanced sample; I didn't want to be talking only to people I knew or just to psychotherapists or only to Ohioans. Most good, reliable intuitives work quietly, and their reputation spreads only through word of mouth. Luckily, networking with reliable professionals who had the requisite connections and experience helped me to expand my reach well beyond my immediate circle.[3]

At one point, I had to ask for more men for my sample, because I was getting only one man for about seven women. This cranked the ratio up a bit, to about three men to every ten women. The ages of the people I interviewed range from thirty-three to eighty, with a large concentration of people in their midforties.

Many of the people are well-known intuitives, authors, teachers, healers, researchers, and consultants. Several have been running their own training programs for years. And many are regularly consulted by physicians, police departments, psychotherapists, government agencies, and corporations. In my sample there are twelve people with Ph.D.'s, nine with M.A.'s, and four with M.D.'s. There are psychotherapists, physicians, nurses, corporate trainers, medical intuitives, engineers, school administrators, finance officers, Spiritualist ministers, computer programmers, artists, entrepreneurs, energy healers, dancers, and martial arts trainers.

Fourteen of the people I interviewed do intuitive "readings" or counseling as their full-time job, without advanced counseling degrees. They have either received some sort of spiritual training or are self-taught. A couple of the people I spoke with refuse to see themselves as especially intuitive. And, finally, a good many of them emphatically do not want to be referred to as "psychics," taking strong exception to the term's association with the world of the occult, TV infomercials, tabloids, and 900 numbers.

From all of my sources I have teased out what I feel are the common, core elements to opening up to psi ability—key components that show up again and again, both in the research and in each practitioner's experience. I've separated out and described these elements, and in the how-to part of the book, I incorporate them into imagery exercises and general suggestions.

And because so many people have looked me in the eye and asked me, "C'mon, Belleruth, do you really believe in this stuff?" and "How could this possibly be?" I've added a chapter that tries to answer those questions. As luck would have it, modern theoretical physics has provided us with an exquisite and comprehensive explanation of how psi works, and there's even some promising research available on the connection between heart-opening imagery and psi. For this section of the book, I lean heavily on the profound thinking of theoretical physicist David Bohm and the brilliant work of the inventor and writer Itzhak Bentov. I've tried to present their ideas in a user-friendly way and have even tested them on my more physics-phobic friends. Nonetheless, if you find your eyes glazing over from the abstractions in this chapter, just skip over it. You'll still absorb its essence by working with the imagery derived from it, which is offered to you in part 2.

The imagery that I've created in the pages of part 2 brings together everything learned from the rest of the book. The guided imagery exercises combine all the concepts, findings, experiences, and methods and present them as several carefully constructed, coherent narratives for you to follow. Record them and listen to them. They work. They'll work even if you skipped over part 1 and couldn't care less about how or why they work.

Sooner or later, either right away or with continued practice, your heart and mind will open to greater psychic knowing.

This is what I know how to do best: construct imagery to help make things happen. Mostly I've applied this arcane expertise to developing imagery that helps people fight cancer, diabetes, arthritis, and depression or that helps them prepare for surgery or better tolerate chemotherapy. I've seen what imagery can do, and I know it to be a pretty amazing tool—easy to use and rewarding in and of itself. But here I apply it to opening up psychic ability and to connecting us once again to the sea of wisdom, compassion, and assistance that surrounds and supports us.

So, in brief, I want this book to help you expand your own native, intuitive ability, comfortably and easily. If you are intrigued but feel a little bit timid or tentative about investigating this terrain, or if you're worried about all of this being a little too *weird* for you, please take some comfort from my own personal biography: my thinking and methods are the product of almost thirty years of committed, ethically bound, professional work. I'm a regular, practical sort of person—a solid citizen, mother of three, married to the same guy for over thirty years, great cook, lousy housekeeper, steeped in the Judeo-Christian ethic, and a registered voter. In short, I'm a pretty grounded, common-sense sort of person who sports a solid, working left brain and who has put her psi ability to good use both personally and professionally.

When all is said and done, I suppose I have two wishes for anyone reading this book. First, I hope it demystifies the workings of your sixth sense to the extent that this ordinary, latent human ability opens up further for you and becomes a simple extension of your everyday perception—a practical tool at your service and in the service of others, without the titillating razzmatazz and melodrama that too often surround it, cheapening and diminishing it.

And, second, I hope it opens your heart a little wider and brings you into a closer contact with the huge mystery, the boundless intelligence, the compassionate, loving wisdom, and the absolute magic that is all around and inside each and every one of us.

PART I

What Psychic Ability Is, How It Works, Who's Got It and Why

Clarifying
Some Terms

As I said in my Introduction, the general territory I'm looking at is what parapsychology researchers call *psi*—the knowing and sensing that overleaps logic, analysis, and rational thought and just shows up. This is called intuition, ESP, psychic ability, telepathy, clairvoyance,[1] high sense perception, and paranormal intelligence.

For my purposes here, I'm much less interested in other aspects of psi. For instance, I won't be spending a lot of time in this book on the phenomenon of psychokinesis (PK), which is about making things happen from a distance with our intention (as in healing, prayer, and the more mundane tricks of spoon bending, table tipping, and the like). And I pretty much ignore the ghosts, goblins, and spirit aspect of things, too (phenomena that also get subsumed under the category of psi), except when some research in this arena helps me make a point about ESP. What interests me most is how we get useful information that bypasses "normal" cognition, perception, or logic.

Clarifying some of my terms will help establish the territory I am talking about. I differentiate among three ways of knowing that often get confused and interchanged. The first is what I call *the knowledge that comes from experience;* second is *intuition;* and third is what I refer to as *psychic knowing.* Even though later on I use the terms *intuitive* and *psychic* interchangeably (particularly because so many people in my study had such an antipathy toward the word *psychic* and beseeched me to please not use it when referring to them), I'd like to distinguish them here.

But first, I'd like to say that I know perfectly well that the word *psychic* has a rather tinny sound, carrying with it some fairly cheesy associations with seances, table tipping, and things that go bump in the night. The negative connotations of the word have been exacerbated by the recent appearance of a spate of TV psychic hot lines of dubious reputation and skill.

The word *intuition,* though still suspect, is on a bit more respectable ground and can be carried more easily into a mainstream venue. When dressed up in its masculine garb and called *gut instinct* or *hunch,* we can take it almost anywhere.

Because of the discomfort that the word *psychic* generates, it often gets downplayed or called by the name of its weaker but more respectable cousin *intuition,* even when *psychic* is what people mean. Several of the people I interviewed, in fact, told me that they avoided using the term *psychic,* even though it probably best conveyed what they could do, because of all of its unpalatable connotations. They preferred calling themselves *intuitive counselors, seers, spiritual advisors,* or *empaths*—anything but *psychics.* (Frankly, I question whether these alternate terms provide a whole lot more positive cachet.)

What was most interesting to me was how much discomfort, embarrassment, chagrin, and repugnance surrounded the term *psychic.* That's a lot of heat on one small word. I suspect it reflects our culture's intense ambivalence toward the whole topic. We're all a little intrigued and embarrassed, I'd say.

All of that notwithstanding, *psychic* really is the word that immediately and unambiguously describes certain things. *Psychic* is the elaborate but sudden "pop" of information that comes all of a piece, seemingly from nowhere. Like intuition, it bypasses rational thinking and just presents itself. But unlike intuition, it also bypasses our five senses and doesn't even bother to dress itself up as a sensory fragment. Because of this, psychic knowing is odder, more striking than intuition, and its appearance might reflect a stronger connection or deeper state of mind. Psychic information tends to be more defined and complex, and it's harder to ignore it or palm it off as a logic-related anomaly. It's intuition—only more so.

It has been my experience that, in spite of the fact that psychic knowing tends to be more dramatic and flamboyant, generally more astonishing and impressive than intuition, it does seem to come from the same preconditions and circumstances. It takes the same methodology to invoke it—only perhaps more of it, in more concentrated doses, over more time. In other words, psychic knowing comes from the same well, only deeper down.

THE KNOWLEDGE THAT
COMES FROM EXPERIENCE

The knowledge that comes from experience can be as fast and as smooth as intuition or psychic knowing, but it's not the same thing. It is the product of logical thinking that has simply become quick and automatic. It's cause-and-effect common sense, accelerated by repetition. Sometimes a dash of intuition is thrown in, too, but often it exists all by itself.

For instance, knowing to cross the street when an innocuous-looking but in fact dangerous stranger is approaching might at first glance look like an intuitive choice, and possibly it is. But it could also result from a combination of memory and analysis, the brain having first made a quick assessment of an atypically stealthy gait, some shifty eye movements, or a certain way of holding the arms and hands and then, based on past experience, associating this particular body language with danger.

Students of intuition call this quick, subliminal processing *chunking*,[2] and it takes place when certain perceptions, through repeated experience, become so automatic as to feel intuitive. Chunking, in fact, often combines seamlessly with intuition.

Clinicians rely on this kind of information all the time, as do seasoned workers in any field. An example of it happened recently with a new client, a beautiful, chisel-featured woman of sixty-one, a successful writer with badly metastasized lung cancer, who was seeking guidance for holistic therapies after a failed course of chemotherapy. The overriding impression that I got from her was that she seemed very, very tired.

While taking her history, I asked her a couple of standard questions about what she had to live for and how much emotional support she was getting. At some point in our conversation, I became aware of feeling a vague sort of discomfort, a very familiar feeling that I'm used to experiencing in my sessions: the best way I can describe it is as a nonspecific sense that something important had been skipped over. I could feel my attention being yanked back to something that she had almost said a couple of questions earlier. But I couldn't place exactly where it was or what it was about.

Invariably when this happens, with barely a conscious thought my interest gets activated, and, before even knowing why, I become like a heat-seeking missile, going back and forth, circling around, scanning for the buried hot spot. At the same time, and possibly quite unconsciously, my artful friend was doing her best to steer me away from the place. And so we danced our little dance for several minutes.

Somehow, my questions began circling around her relationship with her husband of thirty-six years, gently poking and prodding here and there. With each of her answers, she dodged me elegantly, offering graceful, oblique responses, couched in her impeccable manners.

Our little pas de deux finally resolved itself when I leaned forward, elbows on thighs, and asked, "So, is it fair for me to assume then, Jane, that even though your husband is a good man and he's very worried about you and he wants to do everything he can to help you and keep you alive, you don't really experience him as a source of emotional support?"

Her eyes widened, her mouth dropped open, her breath caught, and she very quickly said, "Oh, I would *never* say *that!*" I leaned forward with my best conspirator's smile and whispered, "I *know*. That's why *I'm* saying it." Before she could help herself, she laughed out loud, like a girl, our eyes made contact, and the connection was made. In that moment, the tension between us dissipated, the ground rules shifted, and we both knew that from then on we'd be telling each other the truth.

And so it was no surprise to either of us when she began talking about how hard, how wearying, it was for her to be married—that perhaps for her, the solitude and independence of single life would have been a far better choice, that even when her husband tried to be helpful, to her it just felt like one more set of demands to respond to and accommodate. More than anything, she liked being left alone.

As she spoke, she became visibly livelier, more energized and spontaneous. She looked stronger, freer, less burdened. It was clear to me that she needed to be talking about these things, that it was good for her to be telling the truth.

In this instance, my knowing what to look for and how to guide this woman into speaking the truth about herself appeared intuitive, but it wasn't. It had to do with having sat in my therapist's chair for years and having heard answers to the question about emotional support scores of times before. I knew perfectly well from past experience that even a middling marriage would get a footnote here. And when this marriage didn't, and her husband of almost four decades didn't get so much as a mention, it registered on me subliminally as a major omission and my internal red flag started waving.

And so, too, my tactic for getting the truth out of her had its basis in logic. Her very politeness in dodging me broadcast to me her reasons for not wanting to voice her discontent. Her mannerly resistance told me it would violate her sense of decency and propriety to speak ill of her husband or her marriage. When I intervened I took that into account and gave him credit where it was due.

Again, this was *not* intuition. I had been in this scenario many times before and knew without thinking, from past experience, that this was probably my best shot at helping her to tell the truth while leaving her sense of honor intact. Had I been more heavy-handed with this woman, struggling in a more confrontational way to get her to talk, I never would have succeeded. I knew this all too well because as a younger therapist I'd blown it in just this fashion many times.

So this is the knowledge that comes from experience, arriving as quickly and smoothly as intuition but nonetheless the product of simple logic, married to experience, applied over many years and therefore automatic.

INTUITION

Intuition, on the other hand, has nothing to do with logic, although it can certainly work in harmony with it. Intuitive knowing brings through the normal, sensory channels information that by all accounts we aren't supposed to be getting because it's about someone or something other than us. It's as though our personal boundaries were extended over more territory than just our own skins, and so we pick up data from the environment as if it were about us.

It is intuition operating when a hotel elevator door opens to reveal a man who looks perfectly harmless but nonetheless we find our bodies bristling with alarm, *as if we were presented with concrete, external danger.* The feeling, in fact, might be so compelling that we may actually decline to enter the elevator and instead fake a gesture of having forgotten something and needing to go back to our room to retrieve it.

We are experiencing intuition when the phone rings and we get an irrationally happy, optimistic, expanded feeling, as if something good were about to happen as a result of the call, or when, holding an unopened letter, we have a feeling of sadness or dread because our senses have somehow registered that bad news lies inside, long before our eyes have actually read it. (This needn't be about life-or-death matters. Just yesterday my stomach sank as I held an envelope, and, lo and behold, inside was a notice raising my office rent by fifty dollars—not exactly wonderful news, but not the end of the world, either.) We are experiencing intuition when, greeting a colleague for lunch, we get a sudden feeling of pressure behind the eyes and nose, just an echo of discomfort, that is, in fact, our companion's sinus headache.

In my clinical setting, intuition helped me out with a man who came to see me for intense anxiety. He was a thirty-seven-year-old executive who had just moved to town with his young family to take an important new job. He said he was so anxious he couldn't concentrate, to the extent that he was having trouble taking hold of his new responsibilities. As he spoke in his very rapid, clipped, cerebral way about these things, I felt a deep sadness coming up in me. I more or less dismissed the feeling and went back to paying attention to what he was saying, but the sadness returned right away, very deep and very achy, like old grief. Again, I cleared my mind, and again the feeling came back.[3]

Finally, I interrupted him to ask, "Do you think you might be sad about something? Could you be grieving over anything right now?" He looked a little irritated by the interruption, said no, he didn't think so, and continued to talk about his worries about performing on his new job for his new boss.

I know enough not to argue with people about what I think are *their* feelings, so I just continued to sit with him, quietly holding what by now I felt pretty certain was *his* grief, and I just listened. Within a matter of minutes, his talk came around to two people he'd left behind, the closest male friend he'd ever had and his old boss and mentor, a kind and nurturing man who'd been like a father to him. Because he'd never had such nourishing relationships with men before, these two people were especially dear to him, and he missed them terribly.

Soon he was sobbing deeply and, at the same time, laughing and saying how great it felt to be crying. In addition, he expressed surprise that these feelings had been inside of him all along. When he left my office, about half a tissue box later, he said he felt wonderful. His anxiety had disappeared, along with the lid he'd placed over his grief. Through intuition, I'd picked up his feelings in my own body.

So this is intuition: when, through our own sensory apparatus, we pick up feelings, sensations, perceptions, and emotions that are not ours but belong to someone or something else or that are just plain hanging in the air. Our boundaries are extended to include more than just us.

PSYCHIC KNOWING

My distinction between intuition and psychic knowing is this: intuition is a natural extension of normal, sensory perception, going beyond the individual boundaries of our skin and picking up what is happening in the environment or in the hearts, minds, and bodies of others. It's a greater sensitivity or empathy than we might normally expect, but it doesn't feel extraordinary in any way. It's our same old senses, just stretched over a larger terrain.

On the other hand, what I'm calling psychic information is a sudden, cognitive pop, an instantaneous awareness of a whole idea, sometimes a whole set of ideas or a complete conceptual system, that bypasses anything we would consider to be the normal process of thinking. These pops—sometimes instantly apprehended, sometimes first spoken aloud and later understood—will later strike us as odd, although at the time that they are popping, they feel perfectly normal and natural. They are the stuff that has us asking, "Where on Earth did *that* come from?"

Apocryphal stories of great discoveries come from this territory that I'm calling psychic. Archimedes' "Eureka!" may be the best known, but author Philip Goldberg has a nice description of Nobel laureate Melvin Calvin's sudden discovery in this way: "Calvin . . . was sitting in a car, waiting for his wife to complete an errand, when the answer to a perplexing inconsistency in his research on photosynthesis dawned. [He] wrote of the discovery, 'It occurred just like that—quite suddenly—and suddenly also, in a matter of seconds, the path of carbon became apparent to me.'"[4] This is the kind of cognitive pop I'm calling psychic.

I can offer a less earthshaking example from my own clinical work, one of the first times I became consciously aware of the value of these pops on the job. It happened almost twenty years ago with a woman who was suffering from what we would now immediately identify as post-traumatic stress disorder (PTSD). There wasn't a name for it back then, and we used to treat it the way we treated everything else, with traditional, psychodynamic techniques.

She was a tall, attractive, brainy young television producer with a wildly curly head of auburn hair and a very offhandedly funny way of talking about herself. I liked her enormously right away.

She made it clear to me from the start that she was *not* the kind of person to be coming to a therapist for help, but she'd been in a terrible car accident the week before and hadn't been able to sleep since. The accident had left her in a kind of agitated stupor, emotionally flat but at the same time very anxious and hypervigilant. She couldn't cry and she couldn't sleep. And her concentration was so compromised that her work was starting to deteriorate.

She would not take medication, having come from a family with a long history of drug and alcohol abuse, but she was so agitated and was getting so punchy from lack of sleep that she knew she had to do something. For her, seeing a therapist was distasteful, but it was better than taking pills.

She told me that she, her fiancé, and the college intern she was supervising at the TV station, a sweet young woman she was very fond of, had been coming home from a party when the car had suddenly spun out of control, finally colliding with a telephone pole on the other side of the road. Her fiancé had been driving. She and he were unharmed, but Jennifer, the intern, who'd been sitting in the back seat, was killed instantly.

I asked all the questions I knew to ask. I explored her family and social history, looking for underlying issues that perhaps were set off by the accident. I asked her about her relationship with her fiancé and her young intern, looking for unresolved conflicts. I established a good, strong working relationship with her (easy to do, with our ready-made simpatico). I offered her behavioral techniques and relaxation exercises. And I tried to help her get more in touch with her feelings. I did everything I knew to do. Nonetheless, after two sessions, she was no better off, and I had nothing left in my bag of clinical tricks. In spite of my efforts, she was now visibly worse off—more sleepless, exhausted, and strung out than ever.

I remember very clearly sitting across from her during that third session, seeing her tense, weary face, wishing I could help her, *liking her so very much,* and realizing that I hadn't a clue what to do next. This sense of helplessness was probably one of my least favorite feelings in the whole world, right up there with jealousy and shame—so unpalatable to me that I rarely acknowledged having it, even to myself. But this time, I did.

Suddenly, out of my mouth came words I hadn't consciously thought or chosen. They just popped out of my mouth so that I literally heard them for the first time when she did. I asked her if she was having any recurring images from the accident.

Recognition lit her eyes, and she got a slow, queer, mirthless sort of smile on her face. Yes, she said, come to think of it, she was. She explained that when she'd come to after the crash, she'd checked to see if her fiancé was all right and then she'd turned around to the back seat to see how Jennifer was doing. There she saw her dead intern's face, locked in a bizarre grin, a black hole where her beautiful, white teeth had once been. This was the grotesque image that intruded on her unexpectedly during the day and haunted her several times each night.

Sharing the horror of that image released a floodgate of anguish in her. She choked out the story and cried with wrenching sobs for a long time. She slept like a baby that night, she later told me, and for the rest of the week as well. All she'd needed to do, as it turned out, was to download that hideous image that she'd been carrying around inside, all by herself.

How odd, I thought later, that the key to helping her release all that pent-up grief, horror, and pain was a question *I hadn't even thought to ask*. I had no idea where it came from—apparently not from me and not from her, but from somewhere a lot smarter than either one of us. Wherever it was, I knew it was a good place, and I wanted to get back there again.

So this is psychic knowing—the sudden pop that's cognitive or conceptual in nature, that shows up all of a piece, and that feels very much like grace.

ψ ψ ψ

To varying degrees, we employ all three of these ways of knowing. Sometimes we operate from a sequence of logical judgments that are so integrated into our everyday, working process and happen so quickly that they appear intuitive, but they really aren't—they're based on assessments that come from remembered experience. At other times our boundaries have extended to take in other people and other things in our surroundings, perhaps even the atmosphere of a room, a house, or a whole organization, and we sense these things intuitively, through our own perceptual apparatus. And at still other times, from out of the blue, without benefit of any conscious, logical thought, a fully formed idea comes into our heads or out of our mouths, an awesome psychic "hit" from some mysterious and divinely beneficent source.

How People Come to Be Psychic

Even though I'm primarily interested in looking at how psychic ability develops through opening the heart, I want to take a good look at all the routes to activating psi. This information is fascinating in its own right, but, more important, it has a lot to tell us about what psi is and how it works.

The research, sparse as it is, shows us some things. And the intuitives interviewed for this book certainly had a lot to say about how they arrived at their impressive skill levels. In this chapter and in the ones that follow, I'll be sorting out as many of these factors as I can, and what I can't I'll leave to future research.

But first let me describe some of the more typical characteristics of the intuitives that I interviewed. As I said earlier, these forty-three people were chosen because of their reputations for consistent and impressive psychic ability. These were people with a disciplined, reliable skill that they could call upon at will—folks with impressive reputations and good public track records.

If I had to create a composite profile from my sample, I would find a woman in her midforties with an advanced degree in one of the mental health professions who would say she was born with her psychic ability and could likely point to a parent or grandparent who displayed a lot of it, too.

Other typical features would be a tendency toward bilateral dominance (some degree of two-handedness or two-sidedness as opposed to leading strictly with the right or left side); a stronger-than-average likelihood of being an only child; the presence of some talent and experience in the arts, often in more than one modality (music, dance, art, theater, poetry, design, and so on); a tendency to be either a little dyslexic or else an exceptional student and sometimes both (with a greater-than-usual chance of having a photographic memory, too); lots of experience as a meditator; a powerful need to spend time alone and time in nature on a regular basis; a higher-than-average likelihood of finding broken watches, light bulbs, and small appliances in her proximity, at least at certain periods in her life; a tendency to experience phases of temporary endocrine system dysfunction, popping up and then subsiding, especially an over- or underfunctioning thyroid gland or set of adrenals; the tendency to be a night owl and sleep very little, with frequent interruptions in sleep (more than what aging and menopause might impose); and a greater-than-average chance of having reported sighting a UFO or even encountering an extraterrestrial.

However, let me hasten to add that some of the people I interviewed reported very few of these characteristics. Author Caroline Myss, an intuitive with a strong international reputation, proudly boasts that she has nary a one. So let me quickly reassure you that if you come up short on this odd collection of traits, you are in no way disqualified.[1]

Here is what I have gleaned about the factors that either pre-dispose us to psi or show up alongside of it, starting with the least relevant—the ones you can't do much about or wouldn't choose to replicate—and ending up with the ones that are most applicable to us here, the factors that can be taught and trans-ferred, especially through guided imagery.

WIRED FROM BIRTH

It's true that we are all wired for psi from birth, but it is also true that some of us are more wired than others. Certainly, psi is an inborn, universal, human capability, a natural extension of our built-in perceptual apparatus, albeit one that gets under-played and overlooked in our culture. With focus and aware-ness, however, we can all expand our current level of psi functioning to an impressive extent.

We know from remote viewing experiments at the Stanford Research Institute that almost anyone with a minimum of training and preparation can perform simple psychic experi-ments.[2] Researchers Hal Puthoff and Russell Targ began their now-famous series of studies by using only established psychics as their subjects, but later they progressed to using "or-dinary" people, with results that were just as impressive. They found that when people were instructed to report their most fleeting internal impressions and images and to resist any at-tempts at associating, interpreting, or elaborating on them, they scored extremely well.

But some folks are just born with a naked ability to perceive things that most of us can't, at least not readily. These are fre-quently the people who have other traits smacking of unusual quantities of inborn right-brainedness: bilateral dominance,[3] dyslexia, musical or artistic ability, emotional sensitivity, imagi-nativeness, spontaneity, and strong spiritual leanings from a very young age.

Interestingly, these are also the folks who tend to insist de-
mocratically that what they have is nothing special. This is ad-
mirable, but don't believe them. They just don't fully appreciate
the uniqueness of what has always come so naturally to them.
In addition, some of them have struggled for a long time to
stop seeing themselves as "different," having lived through
enough confusion and pain about their uniqueness during
childhood and adolescence to last a lifetime.

People born this sensitive and opened up can spend a lifetime learning to grow themselves some skin, and often they
have to work hard to become as grounded and reality based as
people like me—just as people like me have to work equally
hard to shed our skins and let go of our strong anchoring
enough to further open our capacity.

Quite a few of the intuitives I interviewed even objected to
my using the word *gift* when referring to this ability, insisting
that psi was an acquired skill, plain and simple, and that they
were no more gifted than anyone else. They warned that people
who liked calling attention to their special "gifts" and "powers"
were often the ones most likely to abuse their talents and keep
people dependent on them, discouraging others from developing their own abilities. And I think this is true. (I eliminated a
few people from my sample who overshot my comfort zone by
sounding a little too taken with their amazingness.)

However, wide differences appear in us from birth. Keep in
mind the analogy to athletic ability: some people are born
loaded with athletic talent; some can teach themselves to be exceptional players, even when starting out with average ability,
because of a lot of commitment and drive; and almost all of us
can learn, without too much strain, to get good enough to play
the game.

But returning to the case for inherited ability, most of the
intuitives I talked to could point to one or two family members
who also had exceptional psychic abilities. Sometimes this

would be a relative with whom they'd spent a lot of time as children, but sometimes it was someone they'd only heard about later as an adult. This latter circumstance strongly supports the nature over nurture argument.

For instance, Lynn Robinson, a full-time professional psychic from Boston who developed her abilities in spite of getting no encouragement whatsoever from her family, learned as an adult about a long-departed grandfather who had had a psychic healing practice. He'd been the family secret.

Similarly, Los Angeles psychiatrist, psychic, and author Judith Orloff, M.D., learned only when her physician mother was dying about her grandmother's psychic healing practice back in their old, Jewish neighborhood of Philadelphia. This had been a source of embarrassment to her upwardly mobile mother, who confided that this was why, when evidence of similar abilities started popping up in her young daughter, she'd enjoined her to keep quiet about them.

Most people seem to have a first memory of a psi experience at about age three or four. There's usually another major flurry of psi activity at puberty—along with all the other flurrying. (As we will see later, shifting hormone levels and expanding psi perceptions seem to go together. Typically, pregnancy, childbirth, and menopause are also times of accelerated psi expansion in women.)

A childhood psi experience might consist of being able to sense what people are thinking and feeling or seeing the actual, energetic traces of thoughts (*thought forms*) springing from people's heads. Some children see colorful, fuzzy auras around people and things and assume that this is the way the world looks to everyone.

Many kids perceive spirits around the house—Grandma or Aunt Fannie or strange visitors in the bedroom after being tucked in at night. Some people say that it was only later, as an adult, that they could understand that the night terrors they'd had as children were probably the result of these spirit visitors, and, because there'd been no family vocabulary for such experiences, they'd been scared out of their wits.

Some children see future events unfolding, either awake or in dreams, and, as children frequently do, they confuse *seeing* these things with *making* them happen. As a result, with a child's logic, some kids shut down their perceptions in an effort to keep bad things from happening to people.

A fortunate few do grow up in a family or community that accepts, values, and understands psychic experiences, has a vocabulary for them, and encourages their development.[4] The Reverend Gregory Kehn, a psychic with a solid track record for accuracy and consistency, based in Girard, Ohio, was such a child, a fourth-generation psychic who was identified and appreciated in his family for having the ability to continue in the tradition of his mother, grandmother, and great-grandmother. He was then mentored by Dana Bailey, another psychic in the community, from the time he was nine until he was well into his thirties. (People like to say about Greg, who is known for his practical, specific, and highly accurate advice, that he can tell you which spark plug is misfiring under the hood of your car.)

But Greg's experience is the exception. It is more likely for very psychic children to shut down because of a negative reaction from a family member. Some of these children are seen as crazy or weird, some are accused of lying or manipulating to get attention, and still others are discouraged in more subtle ways.

I love the way physician and neurophysiologist Mona Lisa Schulz, Ph.D., M.D., describes her mother's reaction when she told her that she'd seen a ghost: "I got the same odd look from my mother as when I asked her about sex. She laughed uncomfortably and got embarrassed. It just wasn't something you talked about."

Of course, these intuitives didn't all shut down, and those who did didn't remain that way. Something or a series of things occurred later on to reactivate their psychic ability and to open them up again. And some of the more extraordinary intuitives never had the option of shutting down their psychic perception because they couldn't figure out how to turn the apparatus off until well into adulthood. With increased maturity and experience, they were able to teach themselves how to contain, manage, and direct their abilities.

But don't get me wrong—not everyone has a tough time growing up with a high psi capacity. Sometimes it just shows up as a talent, a special sensitivity to other people or a fortunate ability to concentrate extremely well. Ken Koles, a psychically gifted healer with a large practice in Cleveland, told me that, in retrospect, the only harbinger of his psi ability that he could look back and identify was his exceptional athletic talent. On his sandlot baseball team, in the exalted position of shortstop, Ken somehow always knew which way the ball was going to bounce and was therefore always in just the right spot to scoop up a grounder.

In my own case, for many years I sported a dubious party-trick talent for mirror-writing in cursive, which I could do with the same speed and accuracy as writing forward (a clear sign, by the way, of some odd wiring and a bit of bilateral nondifferentiation in my brain, a telltale marker of right-brainedness). Typically, as a child I thought that everyone could do this—until I got to college and achieved minor, if short-lived, celebrity status on my dorm floor with it.

So, to summarize what I hope is pretty clear by now, all of us are born with this ability, but some of us are more dramatically endowed than others. We can all increase our psi mastery considerably from whatever point we're starting from, and we won't know how far we can take it until we give it a substantial try. But the evidence also suggests that some people have stronger genetic psi-inclinations than others, over and above the basic human capacity that we all share. This is supported by the fact that other family members have exceptional psi abilities and by the presence of other inborn, right-brained traits.

As Vancouver intuitive trainer and entrepreneur Lee Pulos puts it, "We're all hardwired for this. But some people come installed with some truly great software."

TRAUMA, ABUSE, AND TERROR STATES

If you've ever been in an accident or survived a physical assault, you've had the experience of being in an intense altered state. Adrenalin rushing into the bloodstream creates a hyperalertness and a slow-motion recording of the experience in the brain, at the same time that a certain detachment makes it possible to dispassionately watch and assess the situation as if it were happening to someone else. This highly adaptive response gives us an edge, an extra ability to survive and surmount danger, even though it also means that the traumatic events become seared into our memory traces, revisiting us later at surprising, unwelcome times in the form of flashbacks.

The psychiatric and even the general literature focuses on trauma, especially sexual and physical abuse, as the catalyst for opening people up to psychic experiences. But it's not trauma per se that does this—it's this adrenalized altered state that heightens perception and expands consciousness.

Several of the intuitives I interviewed reported incidents of childhood abuse—between a third and half of them, in fact. And over three-quarters had experienced some sort of trauma in their lives. But childhood abuse statistics run high, and people who have lived to their forties and fifties have frequently experienced some sort of trauma in their lives.

On the other hand, there are many intuitives who insist that they haven't experienced any of these things. Several of the people I interviewed, in fact, described themselves as having been "very lucky" throughout their lives, supporting the idea that being victimized, traumatized, or terrorized is not a *necessary* precondition for opening up psychically. The Reverend Rosalyn Bruyere, a well-known California teacher and healer, suggests that children who are born with an especially strong sensitivity to psi may carry a certain intense kind of light or energy around them that subliminally attracts hungry predators to them, and that this might be what accounts for the allegedly high proportion of psychics who were abused as children. This is a very different spin on the usual causal interpretation, which is that people become psychic *because* they have been abused.

However, there is no question that terrifying situations certainly can and do rev up psi functioning. Psychologist, teacher, and author Helen Palmer talks about the prolonged bouts of anxiety she felt as a civil rights activist in the sixties, when she participated in the highly charged, polarized, and potentially violent atmosphere of various political demonstrations, and how this was a likely catalyst for popping her third eye wide open.

And certainly many intuitives have grown up with one or more irrational, temperamental, alcoholic, or violent parents. As a result, they learn as children to develop a kind of hypersensitivity to the moods and temperaments around them in order to stay safely one step ahead of danger. This adaptive, preternatural alertness to shifting environmental cues becomes the forerunner of their strong psychic skills.

In rarer and more extreme cases, people experience more intense, relentless, and sadistic forms of abuse in childhood. In fact, two of the people in my sample of forty-three were the survivors of a steady childhood diet of Satanic cult abuse, where, thanks to their pathological families, they were given starring roles in ugly demonic rituals. (I know, hard to believe, but true.) These children became adept at protecting themselves during the abuse by altering their consciousness and spending a lot of time out of their bodies in a dissociated, altered state, a kind of "trauma trance." This usually results in an extremely confused, frightened, spacey, but very psychic child.

As you might guess, people who are severely traumatized in this way often have trouble taking charge of their lives, let alone their psychic skills. In order to effectively use and direct their psychic ability, they must first learn to reconnect with their bodies and their emotions and to sort out their boundaries from those of others. They also need to pull the plug on their emotional connection to their abusers (no small matter when these are family members). Without severing these ties, they run the risk of misusing their power and becoming abusers themselves.

Although most of us have trouble relating to this level of abuse, such experiences do provide us with some clues as to the nature of psi and underline the fact that the biochemistry of terror does expand consciousness, heighten perception, and shift the way that time is experienced. Adrenalin propels us into a self-protective, out-of-body trance state, and, in a very speedy and disorienting way, it can pop the third eye open.

Of course there are far more pleasant ways to achieve a powerful altered state and expand consciousness—slower, safer, and kinder to the body, mind, and spirit. I'll be discussing these in the pages ahead. But first, we need to look at an even stranger grouping of psi-conducive experiences because they, too, give us some very interesting clues about the nature of psi.

NEAR-DEATH EXPERIENCES AND
UFO SIGHTINGS AND ENCOUNTERS

Accidents and illnesses sometimes affect people's psi abilities, and sometimes they don't. But a full-blown near-death experience (NDE) does indeed seem to consistently accelerate psychic ability. Professional psi research subject Joe McMoneagle, for instance, told me a typical NDE story.[5]

Back in the late sixties, Joe was overseas as an intelligence officer for the army and was leaving a restaurant with some friends when he suddenly went into convulsions, swallowed his tongue, and stopped breathing. He told me, "All I remember is that I started to feel really bad, and the next thing I knew, there was something like a kind of a loud, pressurized pop, and I found myself standing in the rain on the cobblestone road out-side the restaurant. I could see that the rain was going through my hands, and when I looked over, I saw my body on the ground, half in and half out of the restaurant door, and my friends were hovering around me, thinking I was dead.

"They loaded me into an automobile, and I followed alongside the car, just outside the door on the passenger side, and followed my body into the emergency room. At some point, I started floating away from the scene—it was like floating backwards—and I went through a long tunnel, still moving backwards, until I felt my back bumping up against something warm. I became enveloped by an indescribably warm, loving light, and was more peaceful and happy than I can ever remember being—I can't really describe the feeling. I didn't want to leave. But at one point I was told that I wasn't through and I had to go back. I argued. Then there was an-other one of those pressurized pops, and I was waking up in a different hospital room."

Joe says that after that he began having "spontaneous know-ings." He adds that the experience completely changed his con-cept of reality, and he tried to tell his army colleagues about it. The army's response was to put him in a rest home (this was in 1970, before people were talking about NDEs), where he had to undergo tests to determine if he'd experienced brain damage. Later, however, Joe became one of the first people that the army recruited for its ESP experiments in its newly organized psi in-vestigations in the seventies.

Actually, a variety of researchers (Bruce Greyson, Richard Kohr, Kenneth Ring, and Cherie Sutherland, to name a few)[6] have concluded in separate studies that NDEs somehow stimu-late the development of psychic ability. What they were unable to clarify, however, was whether or not their subjects were ESP-prone to begin with. (Joe feels that he was, that both he and his twin sister were born with very strong intuitive abilities.) From the bulk of the information gleaned from my interviews, I think it's safe to assume that NDEs do in fact increase ESP ability, from whatever baseline ability people begin with.[7]

The most likely explanation for this is that near-death experiences probably stimulate the temporal lobes, the part of the brain that is thought to be involved with producing psi effects.[8] Studies show that when the hippocampus and amygdala, two structures within the limbic system, are electrically stimulated, intense hallucinatory activity is generated. Subjects stimulated in this way report experiencing apparitions, floating and spinning sensations, out-of-body experiences, inner voices, a sense of a presence nearby, and powerful convictions of deep meaningfulness.[9] These responses are typically reported both in people's descriptions of NDEs and in their recountings of their psychic experiences.

These responses also show up frequently in reports of UFO sightings and alien encounters, which, I confess, I bring up here reluctantly and with some chagrin. However, data is data, and, like it or not, over half of my forty-plus, grounded, sensible, no-nonsense interviewees described experiences of either UFO sightings or full-blown extraterrestrial contact experiences.

I was told about red beings with "icy red energy"; gray-white beings with oblong heads and no eyes; shooting blue lights over a New Hampshire landscape; three vehicles doing right-angle turns in the sky for about twelve seconds and then disappearing into the skies above the outskirts of Monterey, California; little green men; red disks in the sky that "seemed alive and with consciousness" in the New York City sky; a "blue-light-body" person appearing in Virginia; pinpoints of light gliding across a Houston sky in geeselike formations; three blue beings inside a red light in the Tennessee sky; and so on. I was pretty amazed.

But whether you can accept these experiences as real or not, there is no question that there is a striking similarity between classic NDE descriptions and these UFO reports. Both describe sensations of floating and motion, experiences of inner voices, and a meaningful (and sometimes, though not always, loving and compassionate) presence.[10]

Studies by psychologist Kenneth Ring show an apparent ESP proneness in people who report either kind of event.[11] He concludes that there is an "encounter-prone personality" and that this personality features a strong ESP ability along with the tendency to dissociate, to generate and remember vivid visual imagery, and to be hypnotically suggestible. British neuropsychologist Jenny Randles came up with similar findings of exceptional ESP ability in her research with abductees.[12]

Both Ring and neuropsychologist Michael Persinger suggest that UFO encounters, like near-death experiences, alter the electromagnetic field in and around the brain, thus inducing considerable temporal lobe activity that resembles a kind of microseizure and leaves people more sensitive to perceiving "alternate realities."[13]

The point to extrapolate and keep in mind here, whether or not you believe in the reality of UFO encounters, is that temporal lobe activity is connected with psi experiences. This is further substantiated by the high incidence of temporal lobe epilepsy, convulsions, seizures, and other anomalies in that part of the brain in people with high psi scores.[14]

YOGA, MEDITATION, AND OTHER RIGHT-BRAIN PRACTICES

We can now move into territory that's a little more in line with everyday reality—ways of opening to psi that we all can relate to and that offer us some practical direction. The most obvious category is the regular practice of certain right-brain activities, such as meditation, yoga, chi kung, self-hypnosis, various martial arts, breathwork, focused performing arts and athletic activity, biofeedback, prayer, and guided imagery. All these activities accelerate the development of psi ability.

Perhaps these practices help because of the sheer discipline their pursuit requires—because of the way they impose a rigorous attentional focus on their practitioners and thus enhance concentration. Maybe they activate psi because of the way they heighten the amount of energy, or chi, in and around the body. Possibly they help because they clear the mind, leaving practitioners a purer channel for accurate, uncontaminated information to come through. Or maybe the mellow neurohormones that these activities produce in the bloodstream, the serotonin high of the flow state, produces strong psi effects. Possibly a meditative activity like prayer strengthens our intentional connection to the divine source of all information.

I think receptivity to psi experience increases for all of these reasons, but the simplest and most basic one is that the right side of the brain is home base for the altered state. This is the territory where sensory perception, emotional acuity, imagination, dreaming, holistic thinking, creativity, and mystical experience all comfortably and synergistically coexist.

And so, right-brain practices such as meditation and imagery will catalyze a quick, deep entry into the altered state. We know from the research that they actually alter the blood chemistry, producing the body's natural equivalent of tranquilizers and antidepressants. And hard-nosed studies with EEG machines, electrodes, and graphs show that practices like meditation, imagery, and biofeedback do indeed change the frequencies of people's brain waves and affect their quality of consciousness.

Scientists Elmer and Alyce Green, for instance, early pioneers in biofeedback and altered state research at the Menninger Foundation, found that their biofeedback equipment[15] could train subjects to shift their brain waves from beta into alpha and theta frequencies.[16] Once in those states, nearly half their subjects reported a very high number of spontaneous ESP experiences, particularly during theta. (This is the state our brains slip into just before falling asleep and while waking up, although some people are entirely capable of walking around and performing everyday tasks well in this mind zone. Seasoned intuitives like Rosalyn Bruyere, Emilie Conrad-Da'oud, and Ken Cohen, who have spent many waking moments attached to electrical leads in various research labs, were found to be in theta during much of a typical waking day.) Theta induces *hypnagogic images,* the sudden, clear, startling sensory images that pop into consciousness seemingly from nowhere. Biofeedback not only makes for greater production of these images but also increases our ability to recall them.

Since those early days, lab instruments have been developed that are far more sensitive than those first used by the Greens. We can now measure with much greater accuracy and discrimination far wider and subtler shifts in brain wave frequencies that are catalyzed by meditation, guided imagery, and certain kinds of breathing practices.[17]

But meditation needn't be defined as an isolated activity done in a lab or on a special cushion designed for Buddhist bottoms; it's basically nothing more than *the exercise of singular, mindful attention in a relaxed but focused and alert way.* Scrubbing pots, drinking tea, playing golf, sketching, or even shining shoes, when done in a highly focused and mindful way, is meditation.

Focused attention alters brain wave patterns and releases serotonin into the bloodstream, leading to a quieting down of ego activity—those executive functions of the brain that include environmental scanning, decision making, assessing, worrying, and analyzing. Once ego activity quiets, the subtler inner cues of psi can become more prominent.

It is in this quiet, subtle world of internal images and sensations that many people first discover their intuitive wisdom. Charles Honorton, an early psi investigator, based many of his early experiments on the idea that psi is always quietly operating but is perceived by most of us only when our attention has shifted inward. This is because psi competes poorly with noisy external stimuli.[18]

So, too, Russell Targ and Hal Puthoff, in their remote view-ing experiments, discovered that their subjects needed very lit-tle training in order to succeed at perceiving distant geographic targets. Aside from a general willingness to participate, subjects needed to develop only a simple openness to picking up faint images and impressions, the kind that are likely to be dismissed or ignored under normal circumstances. These experiments made a strong case that this inner wisdom is operating inside of us all the time but usually gets drowned out by the noisier functioning of the conscious mind.

This reasoning gets support from what most of my forty-three intuitives told me about their personal histories. An ex-traordinary number (92.7 percent) were serious meditators, with several having practiced for decades. Many had also grown up spending long periods of time alone, with only their very rich imaginations for company, or out by themselves in nature, communing with birds, trees, animals, and spirits. In fact, an astonishing 39 percent were raised as only children.

Several also had spent a lot of time engaged in serious, disci-plined training in the plastic or performing arts—music, paint-ing, sculpture, dance, and theater—as well as playing competitive sports—gymnastics, skating, swimming, golf, and baseball. Not surprisingly, all of these practices require intense concentration and thus are forms of meditation that engage and exercise the right side of the brain and propel the mind into an altered state.

Listening to guided imagery will have this effect, too. Over the years I've received many reports of people experiencing unex-pected psychic pops while listening to one of my guided imagery audiotapes. Being immersed in a guided imagery experience, in a state of deep relaxation, can result in the same kind of altered, meditative state that produces crystal clear visions, sudden in-sights, and a mystical sense of oneness with the universe. Though these were not the intended consequences, they happened just the same.

Different forms of meditative, right-brain practices are thus a safe and steady way of producing the altered state of consciousness, the changes in brain wave activity and biochemistry, that produce psi effects. Happily, we don't need to go to the trouble of having adrenalized experiences of trauma, abuse, near death, or, for that matter, encounters with extraterrestrials. Hormones still play a part, but with meditative practices, adrenalin doesn't run the show; instead serotonin and the mellower neurohormones shift consciousness and accompany the changes in brain wave activity.

DIRECT INDUCTION: PROXIMITY TO SOMEONE ELSE'S POWERFUL PSI FIELD

No matter what our parents told us, occasionally we *do* get a free ride, although they were probably right to discourage us from counting on it. But sometimes, just from being in close proximity to the genuine article—a real psychic heavy hitter with strong psi skills and a great big fluffy aura—we can jumpstart our psychic opening. The direct, *energetic* influence of someone with a strong field and more fully developed capabilities—a teacher, healer, friend, or relative—gives us some extra juice, and just from hanging around such people we can hitch a ride on their energy frequencies and accelerate our progress.

This is because consciousness is contagious, and there is a powerful energetic aspect to the mechanics of psychic opening. Along with the alterations in our biochemistry and the shifts in brain wave activity during psi, an even more basic change occurs, *a change in the way that energy oscillates all around and through us.*

In fact, we live in a world of intersecting, interacting energy fields. Through these fields, we are constantly influencing one another in subtle ways. People with powerful energy fields are the ones we describe as having "star quality," "presence," "personal magnetism," or "charisma." In our culture, we're most likely to find them working as actors, politicians, or preachers. Their capacity for holding and emanating large amounts of energy makes it possible for them to engage and influence large groups of people.

Effective healers and psychics also have outsized fields, and when we are in proximity to them, their vibrational frequencies will naturally entrain ours to match theirs, just because theirs are bigger and stronger. So even if they're not trying to, they can "amp" us up to more closely match their own energy.[19]

This is what Dr. Jim Kepner, Cleveland Gestalt Institute teacher and psychologist, was talking about when he told me of his shock several years ago at suddenly being able to "see" inside people's bodies for the first time after less than a day at a healing seminar taught by a healer, the Reverend Rosalyn Bruyere. Although Jim happened to be in a state of great readiness to expand psychically, he nonetheless felt that the main factor affecting him was being able to sit in the middle of an intense and powerful energy field made up of the synergistic combination of Rosalyn's intense field and those of her students. Sixty pumped-up fields, vibrating in sync at a very high level in a relatively small space can pop even a sluggish third eye open.

In fact, most healers consciously heighten and intensify their fields before engaging in their healing work, precisely so that their energy can overwhelm and influence the weaker, more chaotic energies of the diseases attacking people's bodies. (In this sense, healing fits under the psi phenomenon called PK, or psychokinesis, where concrete events are made to happen in the physical world through focused intention, combined with an image of a desired end, along with a coherent flow of energy.)

Certainly my own encounter years ago with an intuitive named Bryan Christopher followed this pattern. Bryan's field was so powerful that he actually had a palpable, buzzy kind of glow around him. Sitting across from him effected an immediate shift in my consciousness and very quickly put me in a crystal clear, highly energized altered state. (This lent new meaning to the old hippie expression, "I got a buzz off him." It's no coincidence that the idiom of the drug culture of the sixties, which so enthusiastically embraced the altered state achieved through chemical substances, used so many electrical/energy metaphors in its vocabulary.)[20]

At the time I saw Bryan, I was a bit of a basket case psychologically, very open to influence, because I was grieving the loss of a very dear family friend who'd been killed that winter by a train while crossing some railroad tracks in his car.

I'd come to Bryan for I wasn't sure what—for some way of making sense out of what had happened, for making contact with my dead friend, for coming to some sort of peace about the loss, and probably for all of the above. I'd been feeling dulled and depressed for a while by then so that when I sat across from Bryan and got an immediate rush of energy, excitement, and clarity, the contrast was very dramatic. My perceptions got much clearer, and I found myself actually seeing in sharper focus and hearing much more acutely. It was obvious to me that something immediate and biophysical was happening, something I could feel not just in my mind and spirit but all through my physical body.

In energy terms, the death of my friend had caused what Rosalyn would call a "disruption in the field." My intense grief had left my energy more chaotically activated and therefore quite malleable and open to influence. Under these circumstances, direct contact with Bryan's more coherent, powerful, and peaceful field had an immediate and profound impact. Shortly after, I began having many more frequent spontaneous knowings and psi events. I'll be discussing these energetic phenomena much more thoroughly in chapter 5; for now, I just want to make the point that this energetic component exists and underlies much of psi's more concrete manifestations.

And indeed, many of the people I interviewed reported a similar experience of a direct induction encounter that was fortuitous and life changing. Of course, because the encounter was often with a teacher, mentor, or healer, other powerful activities such as teaching and healing were also going on that also would have affected psi. But that first, immediate rush of a response, before any substantive transaction could occur, can be attributed to this potent field effect.

FALLING IN LOVE AND HEARTBREAK

Disruptions in the field most often come from the intense emotions of love and grief, which usually are felt all through the body but are centered especially around the belly and the heart.

Many people are psychically activated by the sudden, traumatic loss of someone they love or an intense experience of grief. Such experiences will often catapult a person into near-obsessive searching behavior, a frequent human reaction to loss. A common example of this behavior is when a woman obsessively drives by the house of her ex-husband or repeatedly calls his number and hangs up after she learns that he has just moved in with his new love. Because she feels he is now gone forever, she begins this "senseless" searching behavior in an attempt to stave off grief. Animals who mate for life also will sometimes engage in searching behavior when one of them dies.

Sometimes the searching doesn't stop this side of the grave. The death of a loved one may prompt a call to a psychic, and other worlds may open up. One intuitive in my interview sample told me that when her closest friend was suddenly and violently murdered several years ago, she was beside herself, shaken to the core. She was so distressed—not just at the loss itself, which was terrible enough, but at the way her friend had died—that she became obsessed with finding out how and where her friend's spirit was and whether or not it was at peace. The only time she felt any measure of calm was while she was exploring these questions, and so she spent a lot of time learning about the world of the occult. By the time she found the reassurance she was looking for, she had developed a substantial amount of intuitive skill herself.

But just the intense, unmitigated experience of grief, in and of itself, can open people up to psi. When people can allow themselves to experience the full impact of their pain, without numbing it or shutting it down, they generate a lot of energy around their hearts, and this can spring them wide open.

As with the experience of terror, the raw, adrenalized state of grief activates psychic ability. One healer told me how the heartbreak of getting out of her second marriage was a major force that propelled further opening in her. Another talked about how his heartbreak and anguish from his daughter's kidnapping provided a similar opportunity for growth.

Certainly it's no coincidence that grief is felt as a physical sensation of pain in the heart, right between the breasts, in the center of the chest. Tolerating and breathing through this intense pain builds a tremendous amount of energy around the heart that one can work with later. In fact, several meditations and imagery exercises are specifically designed to help grieving people do this as part of their healing.[21]

The other adrenalized state that can give your third eye a substantial jolt is falling in love. Again, for very different reasons, and with an entirely different set of feelings, the energy around the heart is intense, and the human energy field expands. In the rosy view of those who are madly in love, the whole world is beautiful, along with everyone in it. Sensory perception is sharp and clear, and each day can feel like a glorious, miraculous gift. In short, we're as high as a kite.

This adrenalized state of being madly in love usually lasts for about six months, and during this time we experience coincidences, synchronicities, psychic pops, and enhanced intuitive sensitivity. Later, when the initial brew of adrenalized hormones is traded in for the more sedate serotonin mix of a mellower, more vintage sort of love, a different set of perceptions and experiences take over—more stable but less dramatic.[22]

One healer, teacher, and sensitive phrased it this way: her heart chakra got "blasted open" at each new onset of romantic love, and when she was in this state, she was at her best in mounting impressive demonstrations of psi for her students. She confessed somewhat ruefully that she was a bit addicted to the "high" of those times, which made the rest of her life a little stale, and she was driven to seek out those experiences time and time again.

On the other hand, when she was suffering from the loss of a relationship and experiencing disillusionment about one of her romances, she could feel her heart shrinking and closing down and her energy constricting. Interestingly enough, she thought—and I agree—that this had nothing to do with the basic process of loss and grief. Feeling sad did not shrink her energy; it was her internal litany of self-recrimination, blame, and scolding about being unable to stay in a relationship that shut her down.

So the emotions of grief and of falling in love, both of which pour adrenalin into the bloodstream, heighten awareness, and intensify the energy field around the heart, are powerful psychic activators.

CULTIVATING COMPASSION AND WORKING WITH AN OPEN HEART

Some people develop their psi capacity in a slower, gentler fashion, simply by cultivating the practice of keeping their hearts open and working with conscious compassion. Human service workers who stay involved with their clients and who remain energized by their work, avoiding the burnout that so often visits their colleagues, are people who have been working with an open heart.[23]

And people who are able to sit at the bedside of a suffering relative, staying empathically connected and emotionally available, are sitting with an open heart. When they can experience all the pain, love, helplessness, grief, fear, guilt, disappointment, and anger that illness in a loved one evokes without criticizing, blaming, fixing, withdrawing, denying, or retreating into mindless busyness, they've arrived.

I would define keeping an open heart as this quality of energized presence, a way of staying consciously full of feeling and engaged even (and especially) in the face of suffering and pain—ours and that of those we attend. Although it may initially seem kinder to protect ourselves by closing our hearts down and cutting ourselves off from our feelings, it doesn't really work that way, at least not in the long run. The exhaustion of burnout actually comes from being shut down and disconnected from the vast energy supply that our feelings generate.

Even the more uncomfortable feelings, such as pain, grief, envy, shame, and fury, are a vast energy source, a furnaceful of powerful psychic fuel. We would no more want to disconnect from our feelings than we would want to be unplugged from our vital life force. And, of course, it is the emotions that trigger the neurohormone mix that helps to activate psi.

Mostly, heartful practice is about keeping the heart open to the world around us—to people, places, ourselves, and the divine. It means coming from a place of empathic attunement. It's about seeing the connections, the interlocking webs of energy among people and things, and residing as much as possible in that place of no separation.

The neurohormones that this state of being generates are the rich, mellow serotonin varieties, resulting in a steady, alert, nourishing, full, natural high. The brain wave frequencies become slower, moving down into alpha and theta rhythms, and sometimes the heart and brain even oscillate in sync with each other and the whole body. Emotions become calm and steady, with a lot of gratitude and love woven into everyday experience. Behavior tends to become more patient, generous, and kind.

Really, when all is said and done, this heartful attitude is what distinguishes the work of most of the remarkable people I interviewed. They sit in the seat of the heart. I'll have a lot more to say about this in the next chapter.

To summarize: We can look at all the routes people take toward psychic opening and see many things—inborn tendencies, experiences of trauma and abuse, near-death experiences, meditation and other right-brain practices, direct induction from other psychics, falling in love or heartbreak, and cultivating an open heart.

And we can deduce from this variety of psi-activating circumstances that psi is generated by a whole mix of things over and above a certain amount of naturally inherited right-brainedness: the emotional and neurohormonal changes that span the continuum from adrenalin to serotonin; shifts in temporal lobe activity and brain wave frequencies; and heightened, amplified electromagnetic energy shifts in and around the body. These are the consistent elements that appear to underlie the mechanics of psi.

Setting
the Stage

We've seen the broader life events that promote openness to psi. Now I want to tease out and examine the key components of the actual *in-the-moment* experience of expanding our consciousness and opening the third eye. I want to describe carefully a process that happens in a matter of seconds or less. In this chapter I present all the ways my research shows that the mind sets the stage so that the psychic pop, the intuitive insight, can appear at will.

Later on, in part 2 of this book, I'll be offering you specific suggestions and imagery exercises that incorporate and replicate these elements; they are presented in several easy-to-follow, coherent guided imagery narratives. But for now, I want to spell out the internal process in a linear, logical way, to make sure that the left side of your brain is on board, too.

You could just skip ahead to the exercises and forget about the explanation; it's not necessary to understand how psi works for the exercises to be effective. But I encourage you to stay with me here. A left-brained understanding will better direct your imagination and intention and allow you more latitude for creating your own imagery later on.

In order to help you understand these elements, I list them as if they were separate and sequential, but they aren't, really. They are all enfolded within one another, part and parcel of the same thing. So please remember that once access to psi is firmly in place, these elements will all come into play simultaneously, and the idea of sequencing will become irrelevant. Once practice has made this a natural, integrated experience of daily living, you will need to do very little to consciously gain access to psi because it will have become automatic.

For our purposes here, I've divided the process into two stages. Most of the "work," if you can call it that, is done in the stage we're discussing here—because whatever proactive effort is required, it must be done here—to *actively* create the curiously *passive* conditions that will coax psi into making its sometimes grand, sometimes timid, appearance.

SAME PLACE, SAME POSTURE, SAME CIRCUMSTANCES

Although not absolutely necessary, a certain consistency of location and posture is helpful when first learning a reliable, disciplined way to gain access to psi. Sitting the same way in the same place helps condition the mind and body to activate the intuitive process quickly.

For me, these physical habits happened by accident as I worked therapeutically with my clients. In my office I always sat a certain way, in the same chair, facing in the same direction, and with the same habit of focusing intensely on the person before me. And to this day, even though I no longer need to be sitting in that spot for psi to kick in, it is still the only place where I know for sure that I will *always* receive multiple hits of information in a continuous flow.

Although initially I could achieve this mind state only in my office, later the ability spread out to include other places and situations—for instance, having lunch with a friend who was looking for some advice. I suspect that I could have generalized this capacity even more, but I was never sure I wanted it to be operating all the time.

Several of the people I interviewed reported the same sort of thing: initially it helped to be in the same physical environment or to engage in the same sequence of ritual behaviors to prepare the way for psi. But later on, posture and place became less important as, more and more, they were able to evoke this mind state wherever they needed it.

RELAXING

Although people will experience psychic pops during highly adrenalized times of intense tension and terror, lesser levels of chronic fear actually have the opposite effect and shut down intuitive functioning. Psi is impeded by chronic anxiety, fear, and stress.

So one of the most reliable, not to mention pleasant, ways of activating psi is by deliberately evoking a state of relaxation. Muscle and body tension, as well as conscious worrying and striving, can be reduced or eliminated through deep breathing, relaxed postural cues, meditation, progressive relaxation, or by shifting the focus of attention to pleasant sensory memories and fantasies.

Most of the intuitives I interviewed used some method to initiate relaxation, at least in the beginning stages of their development. Some used two or three deep breaths; others used an affirmation or special prayer; some worked with a sense of settling into their bodies or into their chairs; and some used a symbolic image of a door, a curtain, an eye, a pyramid of energy, or the felt presence of a special helper or guide to initiate their relaxation.

The idea that relaxation is a psi-liberating activity is well supported by research. Too much striving, too strong a need to succeed, and too much of a feeling of responsibility for an outcome will prevent or interfere with psi showing up.[1] With relaxation, we can let go of these things.

So, too, several of the people I interviewed reported that their abilities became less available or reliable when they were feeling tense, tired,[2] frightened, challenged, unsafe, overly invested in the outcome, or too worried about what someone else was thinking. All of this is certainly consistent with the idea that, with the exception of a state of flat-out terror, relaxation is a condition that is very conducive to psi.

In my own profession, I can see that I regularly do certain things to modulate my own internal tension and maintain a relaxed state when working with clients. Usually this involves taking deep breaths, noticing and letting go of physical tension in my body (especially in the neck, shoulders, and legs), while reminding myself to slow down, back up, and stop getting ahead of (or more accurately, *away from*) my client.

So whatever simple methods you normally use to relax and release tension throughout the day are likely to help you here, too, in setting up inviting preconditions for psi to drop in for a visit.

CLEARING AND STILLING THE MIND

Beyond physically relaxing, we need to clear our minds of all the busyness, the "mental noise"—analyzing, worrying, judging, remembering, looking ahead, comparing, associating, and scanning the environment—that we normally do. It is only when the mind has quieted down that the weaker signal of our intuitive voice can be heard.

In fact, psi is probably occurring all the time, but for most of us it is so subtle, so gentle, fleeting, and fragmentary, that it is easily lost in the everyday din going on inside our heads. So it's easy to overlook, overwhelmed as it is by all the stronger signals.

Not surprisingly, meditators have a considerable advantage here. Meditation stills the mind, creating the quiet needed to perceive psi. And, in fact, it's common knowledge that many people who meditate regularly experience spontaneous psychic visions and intuitions in the course of their practice.[3]

In my sample of intuitives, forty-one out of forty-three people, an extremely high percentage, practiced meditation on a regular daily basis. And many of them chose to do some ritual or affirmation or mental imagery to clear and quiet their minds, if only for a few seconds (but sometimes for as long as twenty minutes or half an hour), just before tuning in to their intuitive data.

Brian Fleisher, for instance, an energy healer from Jupiter, Florida, with a special gift for tracking energy, describes his habit of fixing his physical gaze off in the distance and at the same time focusing inward to start his process of seeing. Laura Chapman, a psychologist/healer from Cleveland, describes going into a "nonthinking state, a suspended, open place, where I'm empty of my own process and the witness in me comes to the foreground. . . . My mood is clear, open, and nonattached, with no strong emotions." Terrye Powell, a Scottsdale, Arizona, psychic, describes having a sense of tuning out the world as she knows it and going into "a different frequency."

I, too, believe I've come to practice a kind of meditation in my work as I've relaxed into my practice of psychotherapy. The focus of my attention—the object of my meditation, so to speak—is my client at the moment, and because of my intense absorption, my mind clears itself of much of the noisy debris that normally rattles around in it. I'm sure this is why my mood always gets peaceful and calm when I begin my work, regardless of how agitated or upset I am just moments earlier.

This approach, of course, applies to *any* focus of attention—the clay you are sculpting, the bulbs you are planting, or the plumbing you're repairing. Anything that clears and stills the mind is another psi-conducive precondition that makes it easier to hear the timid, whispery voice of intuition.

CREATING SACRED SPACE: SPIRITUAL ATTUNEMENT

Another element that seems to be key is the deliberate carving out of sacred space: the establishing of a separate, uncontaminated state of mind or even an actual physical area for tuning in to psi. By setting a place apart and defining it as spiritual, we are able to enjoin our psychic ability to come from the highest part of ourselves, the very best within us. This deliberate setting of a boundary between the sacred and the profane, the profound and the ordinary, and then stepping consciously into the sacred space was seen as extremely important by many of the people I spoke with, even some rather secularly anchored, hard-nosed, professional types.

Many people use ritual, prayer, symbolic imagery, or some kind of spiritually based concept to invoke a special kind of purity or holiness in their work. Typically, one Cleveland counselor, Mary Sherman, begins each of her psychic reading sessions by silently praying, "Grant me third-eye vision and the wisdom, knowledge, and skills to know what to do with it. Let me be a channel for healing, with light and love."

The Reverend Gregory Kehn, a psychic reader in the Spiritualist tradition with a substantial following in New York, Ohio, and Florida, always begins his readings with a rather traditional-sounding prayer, intoned with the singsong cadences of repeated usage: "Dear Father God and all other guides, help us to walk the pathway of life that we may accept and understand all obstructions before us. May we deal with them in the highest and best way, and may we be guided by Thy hand, Thy sight, and Thy understanding. Amen."

Santa Fe intuitive Bryan Christopher begins his first consultation with someone by offering a rather lengthy blessing, and thereafter he simply blesses the person and the session, naming the person he is speaking with, the date, and the city. He once told me, "This is sacred work. Sometimes I'm in the valley of the shadow of death, and I know it. I take people's hands and walk with them through it. But I go in safe. I have unequivocal, absolute trust in that. There's something here that I've always felt is divine, and divinely protected."

Several of the people I interviewed felt they were in constant communication with spirit guides.[4] Most saw their information as coming from a divine or spiritual source of some kind. Even those who used scientific "energy" paradigms to explain the source of their knowing, when questioned further, offered a rather spiritual-sounding definition of energy, characterized by a kind of godlike, universal protointelligence.

Many were quite literal in their ideas about sacred space. For instance, one woman begins her psychic work by defining sacred space with certain patterned movements of her arms and hands. She calls these "astral geometries," and they are followed by a very specific invocation: "I am the light. The light is within me. The light moves through me. The light surrounds me. The light protects me. I am the light." This is followed by a prayer: "Allow me to serve, to be pure, and to help in the best way possible." She uses this sequence every time she sits down to give a client a psychic reading.[5] Once the reading is over, she just as definitively closes up the sacred space and steps back into everyday life with a thank-you and some closing energy work for grounding.

Possibly the most complex and elaborate system for ritually carving out sacred space comes from San Diego spiritual advisor Johanna Caroll, who, before each of her telephone counseling sessions, performs a very labor-intensive ceremony. She lights a candle, then incense, and then she burns sage, which she carries in a circle around the chair she sits in and then around the perimeter of the room to "close the space and make it sacred." This is followed by a whole series of imagery exercises designed to invoke guidance, protection, and clarity in her work.

Other intuitives use images of descending cones or pyramids of light, energy, or sound to surround them and define a separate space before they begin their practice of seeking out psi.

Ken Koles, a Cleveland healer with a Ph.D. in holistic health sciences, uses an eclectic combination of tools for carving out sacred space. When I asked him where he thought the information came from, he shrugged and replied, in his unique blend of practicality, spirituality, and droll humor, "Well, you know, God is everywhere, in all of us. God is like the Internet."

Ken told me that when he works in his healing practice he is in dialogue with a whole bevy of spirit guides surrounding him, and he frequently prays for help and guidance as he goes along. He often begins his sessions using a device taught to him at the School of Spiritual Insight Training in Lily Dale, New York. He envisions a divine white light entering his head from somewhere above him. Sometimes he invokes the archangels Gabriel, Raphael, and Michael to help him out. "Sometimes you gotta get the big guys in here to get the job done," he explains.

Another very sensitive and attuned psychic, ceremonial artist Cynthia Gale, checks behind and to the right of her to hear and feel the fluttering of wings that lets her know divine guidance is available to her. However, she tries to inhabit sacred space as much of the time as possible and therefore surrounds herself with sacred objects and sacred ceremony in most everyday aspects of her life. Not surprisingly, she receives psychic information almost continuously.

Certainly, in my own work as a therapist I have come to see the space of the healing relationship itself as sacred, special, and separated from the contaminants of everyday life. And even though I have no specific ritual that I use in any consistent way, in a pinch I've been known to use protective imagery, say a prayer, or burn a bit of sage to purify my office.

The practice of setting aside sacred space calls to mind the ancient Hebrew directive that I grew up with, "*l'havdil bayn kodesh v'chol,*" which instructs humans to distinguish between the holy and the ordinary. I suppose that until such time as we are so perfected that every moment is sacred, we will need our rituals, prayers, and images to help us maintain purity of purpose and action.

As a therapist, I've come to believe that my primary job is to keep the container, the sacred space of the relationship, safe and clean and filled with my highest intentions so that my clients are free to tell the truth about themselves and, in so doing, to heal and grow. I like the simple, clear way that Colorado healer, teacher, and author Ken Cohen puts it: "If you interact in a sincere way, there is a movement toward healing." More and more, I've come to trust in the magic of the container, the sacred space of the work.

And the magical nature of the space is healing to me, too. Many times I enter my office a bit of a mess—distraught, preoccupied, angry, tired, put upon, or just plain wishing I were already on my vacation—and within minutes, even seconds, I settle into a calm, focused, present, clear, and energized state. So whatever the magic of that space is, whatever light or energy or grace enters it and fills the container, it helps me as well.

And the magic of the space allows me to see what I've come to think of as the *hidden splendor* of my clients. Even when their beauty and light are hidden under some rather dingy and decidedly unglorious human trappings, each one of them becomes beautiful to me in the energy of that special, glowing, sacred space. This of course applies to all of us, in any kind of work: by shifting our way of looking, the materials we work with, animate or inanimate, are transformed into something beautiful.

Almost as if to underline this idea of hidden splendor, about ten years ago I began seeing auras around the heads and shoulders of my clients. At first I thought I was having a visual problem. I'd blink and refocus, but then the glowing, whitish border around them, anywhere from three to eight inches wide, depending on the person, would reappear. Years later, color came into play, and I saw that some people seemed to consistently carry more green-blue, others more pinkish colors, and some had darker, brownish places here and there. Colors would vary, depending on what was going on with their health or emotional state at the time, but most people seemed to have certain basic, signature hues. In the beginning, though, and for quite a while afterward, all I saw were these bright, whitish glows, of varying size and intensity.[6]

These auras have come to act as a kind of meditative cue for me. If I feel myself getting distracted, irritated, or impatient, I'll refocus and look at the aura. Seeing auras necessitates relaxing the eyes into a soft-focus, off-center, night-vision kind of looking. So this way of seeing always manages to return my wandering brain waves back to the mellower, more relaxed, benign alpha state and away from the more agitated frequencies of beta.

And, of course, seeing that glow is the perfect reminder to me that my client and I share mutual ground in sacred space. The visual cue of the aura takes me back into the focused, clear, *present* state that I want to be in to do my work. So sacred space is indeed fertile and safe ground for cultivating psi.

BELIEF

Another powerful component in the operation of psi is *belief.* Some of the earliest parapsychology experiments showed that people who believe in the reality of ESP—interestingly enough, they are referred to as "sheep" in the literature—actually do better on ESP tests than those who don't believe in it, who are called the "goats." And goats do more poorly than chance would predict, an effect that's been named *psi-missing* because it supports the importance of belief as a factor, since otherwise, the goat findings would match random chance, not score below it.[7] So it's best to approach psi with a modicum of belief or at least some openness to the possibilities. Being around others who believe in psi is one way to enhance belief. Paying attention and tracking "hits" is another.

The importance of belief as a factor was borne out in the research of British clinical psychologist Kenneth Batcheldor, who looked at how belief is amplified in groups when members share it. He studied the psi-conducive synergy that takes place in groups where both *unwavering belief* and *heightened expectation* are present. In his experiments, this dynamic combination produced unusual, PK (psychokinesis) phenomena such as the tipping and levitating of tables, strange knocking sounds, the movement of objects, and, strangest of all, the appearance of a spirit visitor named Philip, who, like Pinocchio, started out as a deliberate fictional creation of the people in the experiment but took on a life of his own and was eventually observed by several members.[8]

Similar findings were produced by Colin Brookes-Smith[9] and by A. R. G. Owen[10] at the New Horizons Research Foundation in Toronto. This documenting of the reinforcing effect of a whole group's belief supports the idea that attending intuition support and learning groups can be a valuable way for people to enhance their psi skills.

Anne Armstrong, a woman who, along with her husband, Jim, initiated one of the first respected intuition training programs outside of the Spiritualist tradition, always began her workshops by asking participants for stories of their psi experiences, because this reinforced everyone's belief system. Lynn Robinson, a well-known Boston intuitive, does the same thing in her psi training sessions.

Anne Armstrong also has a practice of asking repeatedly in her readings, while she's receiving her information, "What do we need to know about this?" or "What is the significance of this?" and then waiting for—and getting—her answers. This combination of requesting information and waiting for the answers with absolute assurance that in a matter of seconds they will come strikes me as a powerful way of combining unwavering belief with heightened expectation.[11] This kind of clairaudient dialogue is also one of the methods employed by Phoenix intuition consultant and author Victor R. Beasley, Ph.D.[12]

Dr. Vivian Bochenek, an osteopath and healer with a large practice in the Cleveland area, uses a similar process but over a longer span of time. She might pose a question in her mind about a puzzling diagnosis, "What is this?," and then, she says, "I hold the question in my mind and in my body, and then later, maybe falling asleep that night or the next morning in the shower or driving somewhere, the answer will just drift through."

One of my favorite quotes regarding belief comes from the extremely quotable Mona Lisa Schulz, M.D., Ph.D., who seems to favor hockey and pool metaphors. In describing what she feels is required to gain access to psi she says, "Sometimes you just have to suspend disbelief—you can't win if you don't shoot the puck." The combination of intention and belief does the trick, and, if it doesn't, "You just keep on trying."

Medical intuitive Caroline Myss states repeatedly that this ability is a simple extension of normal perceptual abilities, and, because it is nothing special, it shouldn't require any special belief—it just *is*. I see this "no big deal" attitude as another way of affirming belief.

Belief isn't absolutely necessary. I certainly didn't come to my clinical practice with strong expectations and beliefs that intuitive and psychic insights would show up to assist me in my work, although neither did I disbelieve in them. My present belief developed very slowly and over many years from repeated experience, which eventually had an impact on my neutral but open attitude. The more that psi occurred, the more belief I developed, and, conversely, the more belief, the more psi. I suppose the important thing was that I was open enough to let the psychic pops and intuitive insights register on my awareness when they did occur.

Nowadays, I count on psi-based assistance in my work and even take it for granted, which, I suppose, is the ultimate form that firmly installed belief takes.

INTENTION

Whether stated aloud or in silence, in the form of words or images, clear intention is extremely important. Most of the people I interviewed were very conscious and deliberate about either giving voice to their intention or asserting it silently to themselves. Sometimes the intention would take the form of an image, projected in the mind's eye, of the process working well. Many had crafted a personal statement of their aims, which sometimes took the form of an affirmation or prayer that they used in a repeated, ritualized way to invoke their awareness of psi. Several of these have already been quoted in the section on sacred space. But whatever form it takes, intention is critical; it's the coherent force that shapes the energy of the field into the desired outcome.

Practitioners voiced their intention not only at the beginning of a session with a client but also at moments when they felt stuck, confused, or in need of extra help. A woman who expressed her wish to be at her best to serve might repeat her intention several times, in her mind or aloud, during a particularly difficult or confounding session.

A curious paradox operates here, one that everyone familiar with the operation of psi knows quite well: the mind state that is needed to heighten receptivity to psi is one of *intention without striving*. There is a conscious, deliberate setting of intent; the desired goal is declared, internally or aloud. But rather than accompanying this with the usual tension, effort, and proactive striving that most of us generate when we want to *make* something happen, one shifts instead into a state of relaxed, receptive waiting for the information to show up. Belief breeds simple, relaxed expectation.

Generally, it's a good idea to voice intention in a broad, open-ended way, avoiding aims that are too specific. Many people like to ask simply to be of service to the other person's greatest long-term good, whatever that might be. By not presuming to know what that good is, they avoid falling into preconceived notions or attachments to certain outcomes (obviously easier to do with strangers than with loved ones or oneself). This leads to a willingness to go along with whatever information comes up, even if it makes no initial sense, and this approach ensures more accuracy.

Nearly everyone I heard from emphasized the need to be clean and clear in their intention, stressing the importance of sorting through their motivations in order to get their own personal agendas, distortions, wishes, and fears out of the way. Often their statement of intent aimed for this very thing—the ability to keep the work pure by keeping their egos out of it.

Egoless intention became important in my therapeutic practice as well. After several years of working with clients, a lot of the muddy motivation that had infused my earlier work had mostly rinsed itself out. With the increased mastery, confidence, maturity, and skill that came from age and experience, I was far less likely to do things out of a desire to prove myself or a need to heal my own psychological wounds or to create a feeling of being powerful, influential, or in control. Earlier on, in the way that happens with beginners, these needs sometimes pushed up against my desire to help, and I know that at times they confused and distorted my efforts. They still do when I'm tired, vulnerable, or distracted.

Here psychotherapists have the advantage of being trained to examine their motives with brutal honesty in an ongoing way as a regular part of their work. My true, bottom-line intention was to be of good use to my clients, to help them get from A to B, or to achieve whatever was in their best interest. And, paradoxically, the more experienced, relaxed, and knowledgeable I became, the more I understood that I might not know exactly what that best interest was.

Entering psychotherapy as a client is one way of getting cleaner and clearer with intention. Many of the people I interviewed at one time or another had consulted a therapist to work on their own personal issues as a way of maintaining a check on their clarity, authenticity, and motives. Examining their own process in therapy helped them understand their characteristic distortions, which in turn helped them keep the information clear and nonattached.

Mary Jo McCabe, a popular and respected Baton Rouge clairvoyant, author, and intuition trainer, talked about the benefits that her personal work in psychotherapy had given her and how the process helped her sort out which psychic information was about her and which was about her client.

At the same time, as Caroline Myss is quick to point out, there should be nothing special about keeping our intention clean and clear when we tune in to psi; the intention in *any* endeavor should reflect an honor-bound code of integrity and a scrupulousness about not using any of our personal powers, talents, or skills to harm, weaken, or manipulate others. This, she emphasizes, applies to anything, not just the harnessing of psi. It is simply the way we all should be in the world.

OPENING THE HEART: GRATITUDE AND UNIVERSAL LOVE

Finally, the energy of the open heart, with all its attendant empathy, warmth, and feelings of human connectedness, is a powerful breeding ground for psi. The noted researcher Richard Broughton, Ph.D., director of the Institute for Parapsychology in Durham, North Carolina, reports that it's no secret among psi researchers that the best ESP results come from labs and researchers who can provide a warm, supportive, and caring atmosphere for their subjects.[13] He also notes that the nurturing, feeling tone of the psychotherapist's office has become a rich source of striking anecdotal evidence of ESP.

This is why John Carpenter, a psychotherapist and psi researcher, designed a study that worked to replicate the emotional intensity and connectedness of group psychotherapy sessions in his psi experiments, finding that the higher the level of emotional depth, intensity, and mutual group involvement, the more likely the group was to be on target with the telepathic images that were being directed toward it.

Philosophy professor and author Michael Grosso, in his in-depth studies of world-famous spiritual healers and psychics such as Padre Pio, Sathya Sai Baba, and even Jesus, found his subjects shared an ability to feel deeply, and he writes of the ease with which they could laugh and cry.[14] He contends that their natural, spontaneous openheartedness and emotional availability predisposed them to strong psychic ability, along with their other right-brained traits: a sense of humor, artistic talent, metaphoric thinking, spontaneity, natural authority, and charisma.

And, in fact, most of the intuitives I spoke with described themselves as emotional, sensitive, empathic, and attuned to feelings. Most said that they were born this way; several reported that they had become even more so by consciously working to open their hearts and become more compassionate toward others, either through psychic and spiritual insights, through their personal work in psychotherapy, through the experiences of their lives, or through a combination of these. Sometimes an important loss, disappointment, failure, illness, or trauma shattered some insular closedheartedness—broke their hearts open, so to speak—or in some other way opened them up to greater feeling and compassion.

Many described an openheartedness, an expansiveness of spirit, that occurs inside of them when they are alone in nature. For several people, solitude in nature was something they regularly craved, especially when city living had deprived them of it for too long and had shut down their hearts and minds.[15] Cynthia Gale talks eloquently about her joy at connecting with the animals, trees, earth, and sky and her attunement with all the languages and songs of nature. She and many others told me that it is this sense of connectedness to all things that is the essence of her open heart and her psychic ability. (Cynthia even hears *houses* talking, and she swears that my kitchen chortles when certain family members pass through it.)

Johanna Caroll talks about feeling waves of warm energy moving through her heart while she performs her standard twenty-minute ceremony designed to prepare her for a client counseling session. During one part of her ritual, she sees herself as "breathing in love and [with the outbreath] releasing fears from the past; then breathing in love and releasing ego and all judgment; then breathing in love and releasing the pain of past relationships." Further, she says, as the session progresses she can feel "a lot happening in my heart, like it's racing. And like it's opening, like a rosebud, so that my whole chest area feels bigger, expanded. It fills up, if that makes any sense."

Psychologist Deborah Rozman, Ph.D., describes the "liquid feeling of harmony" that she feels when she focuses on the area of her heart during meditation, holding her attention there and radiating love and care. Rozman directs the Institute of HeartMath, which is developing research to show that these loving mind states produce highly intuitive insights.[16] Although I'll be spelling this out in detail in chapter 5, I'll give you the short version here.

Because the heart is the most powerful oscillator in the human body, when it locks into the rhythms of this loving state, the rest of the body, including the brain, lines up with it in a state of "internal coherence." These matching entrained frequencies, vibrating throughout the body, produce a deeply meditative, aware state, which generates intuitive insights and deep feelings of peace. "It's as if you can feel your cells rejoicing and more spirit coming into you. You're radiating love out, and it's coming back in at the same time. . . . It's very nurturing," Rozman told me.

In my own work, it was certainly true that over the years I became more and more openhearted and compassionate and less and less judgmental. As my competence grew, and as I needed less and less energy to think about what to say and do next, I relaxed, and my criticalness—of myself and of others, too—began to melt away. In the reassurance of seeing people somehow get the help they needed, I grew less frightened of making mistakes and so less hard on myself. I began to feel I could trust myself, the relationships, and the work itself, and with this my heart was able to soften and open.

In this expanded state I could allow myself the luxury of sitting back and enjoying the *quality of the connection* between me and my clients, the sheer richness of it, as they sat across from me in my office. Bathed in a kind of warm pleasure, a feeling of gratitude for just being there, I could really look at them, listen to them, take them in with all of my senses, and fully appreciate them. In this openhearted state, I could feel what they were feeling, sometimes minutes before they themselves were aware of it. And at the same time I could also see them in a kind of abstract and transpersonal way—as heroic, brave, and luminous, struggling to find purpose and meaning and doing their best to discover and meet the demanding requirements of the soul.

As I heard their stories I would become suffused with what I can only describe as *love* for them, very soft, full, and sweet. Just as Johanna Caroll describes, there was a warmth and expansion in my heart. I was moved and touched by their journeys, by the doggedness and courage that kept them going in spite of very harsh life circumstances. I could see and feel what was difficult for them as if I were experiencing their troubles, even though the particular circumstance might not be difficult for me at all. And I was frequently and easily moved to empathic tears, which, after I got used to their regular appearance, didn't bother me a bit.

And even though their distortions and flaws were perfectly apparent to me—believe me, this was not a blind, flight-into-light state of Pollyanna denial—nonetheless, from my therapist's chair I could see my clients in a larger dimension. It was as though I were seeing them from a detached place, from above the fray, away from tightly held judgments and story lines. From this larger view I could appreciate their beauty and the paradoxes and ironies of our shared, confounding human condition.

In this nourishing state of mind, I was protected from being fooled by my clients' limited view of themselves. In the bright, soft light of the open heart, their hidden splendor was apparent. I could see who they really were. (It is always a dangerous thing when a therapist colludes with a client's limited view of himself or herself. The negative collaboration puts a debilitating lock on the potential for growth and creates an arbitrary ceiling on change. In fact, many clients leave their therapists when, at some level, they comprehend that they've gone as far as that particular folie-à-deux collaboration can take them.)

My professional training also helped me to open my heart. I had a graduate school supervisor, Barry Levine, who early on taught me something profound that has always stayed with me. He told me that if I had no empathy for a client, it was because I hadn't collected enough data. So if I found myself devoid of compassion, my job was to get the missing data.

I remember how this first came up—in regard to a client I was evaluating for the court, a homely young man with stringy, blond hair and grotesquely enlarged, pale blue eyes, distorted by thick lenses. This young man, in a flat, detached monotone, used to tell me how he liked to burn little girls and boys with the lit ends of cigarettes. I would find myself tuning him out in our sessions, wishing I could be filing my nails or filling out forms, and going emotionally flat myself.

Barry hounded me to stay present and engaged, to poke and prod around in my own reactions to this man until I could find in him something genuine that I could connect with. Of course, I was twenty-three years old and much more interested in stoking the fires of my righteous indignation. (Young adulthood, like adolescence, is a time of self-definition, of putting our values in place. So it's a time when a lot of energy goes into pointing the finger and saying to ourselves or to anyone else who will listen, "I'm not like *that!*") But my assignment from Barry was to find my missing empathy.

I can still remember my feelings of disgust and how hard it was for me to stay present with this man. Emotionally, I wanted to bolt (which was what I had been doing by fantasizing about a manicure). With Barry's help, I saw what that was about, and I learned a lot. My emotional flatness had to do with matching his mood, going into a dissociated place that was disconnected and cold, which was in fact where he lived his life. I was feeling his sadism but directed *toward him.* And I could do so because—surprise!—I was capable of sadism myself. By disowning the feeling, I'd disconnected from a part of myself that I needed to stay in tune with and remain responsible for.

And, of course, once I could accept my own capacity for meanness, my own ability to coldly objectify other people, I was able to find a place where we could begin to work together. It was certainly nowhere to be found in his current life. But when he spoke of his childhood, he was able to show me his sadness and hurt, his loneliness, humiliation, and fear. I could see the injured child he once was because he looked it and felt it as he spoke. This was the place where his humanity still resided, before it had gotten pummeled and twisted. I could feel for the child and see the bigger human picture there.

Of course, I would be just as unwilling today as I was then to let this man loose on the street. But that's a separate issue.

I did learn to feel for him. The open heart is all-inclusive. It doesn't comprehend separations, exclusions, and hierarchies of being morally better or worse than others. In the open heart, we're all in this together.

However, this business of opening the heart is not just about loving another person and feeling empathy for him or her. That is a piece of it, but just a piece. My energy healer friends would say that this kind of personal, one-on-one loving is mostly at the second-chakra level, the energy center in the belly that is the seat of our earthbound emotions, our creativity, our sexuality, and our feelings of romantic love.

But what we are really talking about here is *fourth*-chakra business. This is the energy vortex located at the heart center in the upper chest, seen metaphysically as the seat of wisdom and compassion, and the place in the body where the earth energies of the three lower centers meet the spiritual energies of the three upper ones. The heart center is the seat of a vaster, deeper kind of compassion and love-wisdom. It's about *lovingness* rather than just love. It is here that we can begin to glimpse the true nature of the soul and where we can feel our connection to everyone and everything.

And it is here, at the heart center level, that we can begin to grasp *experientially* the complex ideas from theoretical physics that describe how, when all is said and done, we are nothing but vibration in a sea of living, intelligent energy—that although we are disguised as separate, solid matter, this appearance of solidity is only how we appear in the overt, concrete order of manifest reality; at a deeper, truer level, we are all nothing but interconnecting, interpenetrating energy fields, transcending time and space, each vibration containing everything in the universe, each subatomic bit of us a hologram of all that is. This is why we can experience instantaneous, direct knowing. This is where those psychic pops are coming from.

At the psychological level, we can say that when we open our hearts, boundaries dissolve. The ego expands and encompasses more than just the self. The I-thou distinctions, the line between self and not-self, disappears. It is no longer a matter of you and me. I become you and you become me. My energetic field opens, expands, and intersects with yours, and our realities merge. Or, if I carry it further, I merge with my family, my country, my species, with all of creation, with the entire universe.

I now have a different perception of the ancient Hebrew assertion that I grew up with, the core element of every service, "Hear O Israel, the Lord your God, the Lord is One." I was taught from a very young age that this was a critical historical stand against idolatry. I'm sure that this is so. But I think it also expresses this wider meaning, the interconnection and unity of all things, and I'll bet that's the real reason it retains its centrality and power in Judaism.

No one describes this heart-opening experience more eloquently than Dr. Vivian Bochenek, a gifted osteopath, psychic, and teacher with a traditional medical practice. Her descriptions of how she knows when true healing is happening are very moving to me. She says, "The person could be hideous, and I love them. It's a deep sense of love, and not even personal—I'm loving everyone on the planet in that love. It's a deep, deep love. Your heart hurts with love, you want to help them so much. You melt, you're one heart together. You can feel all their pain—it's a feeling of 'we're in it together.' This is what it means to be the Heart of God, the heart of one another."

She goes on to say that it's impossible to have this feeling all the time. "Sometimes, when your heart isn't in it, when you're tired because you didn't sleep all night, and you just don't have it . . . then your intention and integrity have to carry you. It doesn't always have to be some big, ceremonial YES. Sometimes you just show up with your lab coat on and you do your work. And you can make a difference then, too, but it's not the same.

"But when you have that feeling—and you never know when and why it'll happen—it's so blissful and exquisite and filled with gratitude, you're on a heart-to-heart level, and the other person experiences the connection, and that's where the healing can happen—the deep, miraculous kind."

Iris Saltzman, a well-known Miami intuitive, describes her direct and near-continuous experience of empathy both in her openhearted work and in her daily life. Her empathic ability is something she had to learn to shut off, because otherwise the sheer volume of sensation and perception would take too much of a toll on her psyche. She told me, "I become whatever or whoever I read. If I'm with a five-year-old, I become five. If I'm with a flower, I become the flower. I know if it needs water or sunlight. I feel it." Then, over the phone, she proceeded to describe, all too accurately, the dull ache in my perennially arthritic knees.

Sue Greer, a spiritual counselor and healer from Columbia, Maryland (who was tested and studied at age fifteen by the Edgar Cayce researchers at the Association for Research and Enlightenment in Virginia Beach, Virginia), cautions that without the heart being open, there is no empathy in a reading, no compassion, no translation to the human level. "It's just a lot of pretty colors and light. It's not usable, human information."

In a similar vein, Bryan Christopher says, "Seeing through the heart is what heats the information up, makes it hearable, absorbable, usable to the person. Otherwise, it's cold and heartless, just pure light energy. Where I go to see, it's pure and hard and sharp, like a guillotine. . . . The heart transduces it to a human level."

Bryan goes on to say that he sometimes asks people to "close your eyes and open the eyes of your heart to see the pathway of your life." The eyes of the heart, he says, see beyond the "small stuff" and into the big picture. "It's hard to describe in concrete terms, but there's something like a crystal in the heart center. It's like a microchip that holds personal information and universal information. It's like a thumbprint, carrying identity, like spiritual DNA." This is the place where the information is received, he says.

Similarly, Phoenix author and intuitive teacher Victor R. Beasley, Ph.D., says, "The intelligence of the heart is soul-awareness. The soul is a repository for all our life experiences, and it's plugged into Divine Mind, God, Universal Intelligence . . . whatever you want to call it."

Cleveland psychologist and energy healer Laura Chapman describes going through a period in her life when her heart was very constricted, when psychologically her defenses were up and her emotions were shut down. When she opened back up to life, she says, the contrast was stunning. "Then I got it, that if my heart was really open, there was no limit to what I could see. This was huge."

She recalled a time when she was running in her first triathlon and was worried that she wouldn't be able to finish. She began thinking about every person in her life who had ever encouraged her, who told her "Go for it!"—and her heart sprang wide open. She finished in fine style.

This is similar to Vivian Bochenek's description of driving to work, when sometimes she thinks about "all the people, all over the world, who worked to make my car so I could be driving to work, and I'm filled with grateful feelings. It helps me to find my place in things, and I'm awed by the whole mechanism, how we all got here together." Images and thoughts like these feed the energy of that fourth chakra and keep the heart nourished and open.

So sitting in the huge seat of the open heart, filled with feelings of love, gratitude, compassion, and care, is a powerful and nourishing precondition for activating psi.

All told, then, several key components provide a fertile breeding ground for psi: consistent place and posture, relaxation, a clear mind, sacred space, belief, intention, and an open heart.

Letting It Happen

FOUR

Once the ground is pre-
pared with the basic elements described in chapter 3—relaxing,
quieting the mind, creating sacred space, cultivating belief, de-
claring intention, and opening the heart—then psi is very likely
to come calling.

Now I'd like to examine the elements that make up the
mind state *during the actual psychic pop* itself. As best I can, I
will break down the internal experience right at the moment
that the psychic information is coming through.

As with the psi-conducive elements in the previous chapter,
I'll be replicating these in-the-moment elements in the imagery
that I offer you in chapter 6. You'll find that they are embedded
in the imagery exercises so they can allow you relatively easy access to your own richly rewarding intuitive state.

But first, let's take a look at what these components are.
Again, keep in mind that they do not happen in sequence; they
tend to happen all of a piece. But it's easier to describe them
and learn about them by separating them out in this way.

RECEPTIVE MODE AND PASSIVE VOLITION

Shifting from active to receptive mode is a key ingredient in gaining access to intuitive information. Opening to receive psi involves surrender into a very alert, aware passivity. The ability to move at will into this open, receptive mode quickly and easily is the core of the intuitive experience and, for that matter, of all creative experiences. The original meaning of the term *channeling*[1]—now narrowed, distorted, and much maligned—reflects this idea of becoming an open conduit through which information, intuition, energy, inspiration, and creativity can flow.

The importance of moving into receptive mode is supported by the research. In fact, it's the most consistent finding that the literature has to offer us. Opening to psi involves the paradoxical requirement of *actively* clearing the mind so that we can *passively* wait to receive information.

Menninger biofeedback pioneers Elmer and Alyce Green coined the phrase *passive volition* to describe this state of mind, which they defined as a detached and effortless way of envisioning something through deep focus but without striving. Imagining a desired end state creates a fertile field for that to happen.

The Greens found in their experiments that imagery alone was often sufficient to manifest a real outcome; subjects were trained to lower their blood pressure and control many other supposedly autonomic nervous system functions simply by imagining these outcomes. This, of course, is the basis for guided imagery's effectiveness.

Kenneth Batcheldor's studies established that people impeded their psi functioning with what he called *ownership inhibition,* a sense that they were personally responsible for making things happen. When they believed this, they became anxious about personal failure and their psi functioning dropped markedly. But when they were encouraged to believe that the outcomes they desired were not in their control but somehow up to some other agent or circumstance—in other words, when they had a mind-set of passive volition—their scores improved. This is why so many psi exercises encourage people to focus on something outside of themselves—a crystal ball, a deck of tarot cards, an imaginary wisdom figure, or even a paper clip—to "give" them the answers.

And this is why author and psychologist Helen Palmer, the founder and director of the Center for the Investigation and Training of Intuition in Berkeley, designed psi-expanding exercises that had her students focus on a leaf or a rock "to see what it could 'tell' them about a personal situation or problem."[2] In this way, random objects not only served as a mind-stilling focal device to help to capture interior messages on an exterior surface, they also helped to remove the hindrances of ownership inhibition.

Even in Batcheldor's table-tipping experiments, people were far more successful when they addressed the table *as if it had a mind of its own,* asking it if it perhaps wanted to move, than when they themselves tried to *make* it move as a function of their own will.

Many other researchers also have noted that when people felt under pressure to perform or to be accurate or to make something happen, their accuracy declined. All of this supports the importance of staying in the nonstriving, passively receptive mode. To paraphrase the noted psychologist and author Frances Vaughan, trying to make psi happen is about as fruitful as pointing a gun at a flower and commanding it to grow.

Every person I interviewed was acutely aware of the need for this attitude of surrender into receptive mode and was proficient at quickly effecting the detached state of mind that brought the information through. Some, like Iris Saltzman and Bryan Christopher, were able to stay in this open, receptive state of mind almost all the time, with a continual influx of psi. They experienced no lag time between the desire to know something and the appearance of the information. Bryan, like Iris and a few others, had become so at home in the mind state of passive volition that unless he deliberately put himself in "neutral," his psychic sense was fully engaged and he received images nonstop—on streets, in hotel lobbies, at airports, in meetings, and during telephone calls.

This constant flow of information, as you can imagine, is not always a day at the beach. Bryan, Iris, and some of the other people born with strong "wiring" for psi, had to learn the reverse skill: stopping the information at will for their own peace of mind.

Others, like Mona Lisa Schulz, use imagery in conjunction with passive volition. In her practice as a medical intuitive, Mona Lisa provides health information over the phone. Her track record is impressive and accurate. She works by imagining that she is seeing the person in front of her. So, for instance, she'll imagine she is listening to the person's heart, and, in a matter of seconds, she will hear a heartbeat. She then imagines herself watching someone get on a scale, and after a brief pause, she will see the height and weight register. In her mind's eye, she looks at a slide of some tissue under a microscope, and soon she is seeing some cellular pathology. (In spite of the fact that, with an M.D. and Ph.D. degree in neuroanatomy, she has the training and background to diagnose exactly what she is seeing, she prefers not to make medical diagnoses in her capacity as an intuitive. Instead, she reports to her callers what she sees *descriptively* and then encourages them to get checked by a physician in an old-fashioned office visit.)

Another woman, in fairly typical fashion, describes her passive experience of receiving information in this way: "I just let the information come in through the top of my head. It just comes." Another reports, "It's just an idea or image that's in my head. I used to have to ask for it and wait for it to come. Sometimes it would take a while, especially if I was a little nervous. But now I'll just ask and it's there, right off the bat."

I notice in my own practice, too, an automatic sliding in and out of this receptive mode. Sometimes I'm actively thinking and choosing what I want to say or do or I'm thinking analytically about what is needed. At other times, particularly when I'm at a loss, I put my trust in the process of pausing and taking a moment to clear my mind and see what wants to show up. Strange as it sounds, I'll sometimes begin to speak without knowing what I'm going to say, and, miraculously, helpful words and coherent, on-target phrases come out of my mouth. Then I'll get back into active gear and process the ideas with my client. This going back and forth from active to passive and passive to active is very smooth and easy and doesn't look or feel unusual at all.

THE GREAT LEAP INWARD AND/OR BEYOND

Another crucial feature of the experience of psi is its quality of deep inwardness. External perception is temporarily turned off. We are inside, not outside, when the information comes to us. It is as if, by diving deep inside, we traverse and transcend our own interior, winding up in an entirely new, far more vast space—a bit like Alice falling down the hole and finding herself in Wonderland.

For this reason, it's best for most psi trainees to become adept at disengaging their senses from the outside world, at least in the beginning when they are just starting to get proficient. Later, with practice, people are able to be both places— inside and out—at the same time.

So for many, tuning in to psi has a quality of moving more and more deeply inward and downward, as if the eyes and ears were turned outside-in, facing the deep, dark spaces of our inner world. Sometimes people will use an imagery device to help them shift into that interior space, imagining something like a door or curtains or some other entryway that opens the gate into this other territory, this other-dimensional, nonordinary space.

A perfect and very commonplace example of this—shutting out the exterior world and tuning into the deep, dark, interior world of psi—is the dream state that we all enter during sleep. Not surprisingly, psi is very much at home in the world of dreams and shows up a lot there.

This was well established in the ESP dream studies of Montague Ullman and Stanley Krippner (often referred to as the Maimonides Dream Lab studies),[3] where they showed that, while dreaming in the lab, subjects were able to achieve an accuracy rate of 83.5 percent (chance would be 50 percent) for correctly perceiving the picture slides that a person next door was concentrating on. Dream studies tend to yield consistently excellent psi results.[4]

The importance of interior focus was also borne out by the intuitives I interviewed for my study. With the exception of the people with continually wide open psi perception, the people I spoke with had trained themselves to be receptive to psi through refocusing their attention away from external stimuli in one of two ways: either they moved their awareness inward into their bodies (and away from their internal *thinking* process), or they focused on an image that represented some sort of gateway or opening into the psychic dimension—this deeper, quieter, more internal space.

As usual, the more experienced and habituated people were to their process, whatever it was, the less overt effort was required. With experience, access became increasingly automatic and integrated.

Several people, in describing their ways of moving inward, reported that they briefly lost track of external sights and sounds as they attended to their inner cues. Iris Saltzman, for instance, visualizes herself quite literally turning a knob that shuts off the left side of her brain. Another woman reported experiencing the sensation of getting very small and con-densed, as if she were contracting into herself, and then, as if passing through a barrier, experiencing a feeling of enormous expansion and vastness.

For Lynn Robinson, turning inward to tune out external feedback had more to do with giving herself the freedom to ig-nore her clients' reactions to the information she was offering so that she could stay on course, unswayed and undistracted. She was so sensitive to the possibility that her information might cause upset that she needed this approach.

Cleveland psychologist and author Jim Kepner spoke of "a feeling of something opening up behind me, or sort of like falling back into another space behind me . . . almost as if something were shifting in the bones at the back of my neck." In a similar vein, ceremonial artist Cynthia Gale described her experience of psi territory in this way: "It's like having a door open in the back of my head. The door is tiny, but what's in back of the door is huge."

Someone else talked about feeling "a kind of linking into something, a connecting up to something . . . like entering an-other place, but very subtle, hard to describe." Don Treadwell, an Indianapolis minister and intuitive counselor, described his experience as a sense of moving through a very subtle door or a curtain in his mind's eye.

In my own experience as a therapist, it took quite a while to realize that during those moments when I was delivering psi-derived insights to my clients, I was not actually *seeing* the people I was talking to. My eyes were pointing in their direction, but I was not seeing them; I was tuned elsewhere. So I was always a bit startled and pleased to suddenly see the reaction on the other person's face, and to find that my words had hit home.

This looking-but-not-seeing was entirely involuntary. As I examine it now, it is clear to me that this was the natural byproduct of moving my awareness away, into some deeper, quieter, more internal place. It was only from this vast, interior place that I could receive the information that was needed in that moment and allow it to come through.

So having the perceptions turned inward and away from the outside world is an important component of receiving psi information.

SUBTLE PERCEPTION: TRUSTING THE INFORMATION AS IS

Along with a receptive mind state and an inward focus, the experience of receiving psychic information also has two related, critical features: first, a quality of very alert attention to the subtlest and most fleeting of inner impressions; and, second, an acceptance of those impressions *as is*, without assessing, interpreting, embellishing, or noodling with them in any way.

Both are simple skills that can be easily developed. With practice, it is easy to gain tremendous acuity in picking up very delicate, fleeting impressions. Simply by noticing them rather than dismissing them, we can enhance their prominence. We can also train ourselves to leave the impressions alone in an ambiguous, undefined, and unanalyzed state, until their meaning develops in its own way.

In fact, even putting these delicate impressions into words runs the risk of distorting them. Ingo Swann, the gifted artist and often-studied psychic, was one of the first experts to caution against premature labeling, categorizing, or defining psi impressions. He wrote, "The mere action of trying to verbalize what I was 'seeing' was an impediment, because it caused the mind to manufacture far more images than were needed ... flooding the perceptual ESP field with useless and inappropriate information."[5]

Proof of the validity and effectiveness of staying with simple, unelaborated impressions was established by Charles Puthoff and Russell Targ, when they found that anyone could gain access to psi if properly coached. In Puthoff and Targ's remote viewing experiments at Stanford Research Institute, subjects (one of whom was Ingo Swann) were asked to sit in a room and to both draw and describe in words the randomly chosen locations that were, at the same time, being visited by someone else on the team.

The subjects were told to observe and report their most *fleeting* impressions and images and to withhold any attempts at analysis, interpretation, or elaboration on them. The results were impressive; their accuracy was so far beyond chance that ample evidence of psi in the average citizen was well established.

Puthoff and Targ broke new ground when they spelled out how to observe psi properly. First, they underlined the importance of paying attention to easily ignored, subtle fragments of impressions, regardless of how vague and momentary they were. In addition, they found that scores improved when subjects gave more weight to certain impressions: to their first impressions; to their more spontaneous and surprising impressions; to impressions that were multisensory as opposed to merely visual; and to impressions that carried an emotional component. When subjects were coached to pay attention to these things, ordinary citizens became as proficient at remote viewing as the people identified as psychic—and in a very short period of time, usually a couple of hours.

Perhaps the most important contribution these studies made, however, was in pinpointing the confounding influence of *secondary elaboration*. This is the natural tendency of the mind to make assumptions, interpretations, and elaborations, over and above the raw psi impressions—a common cause for error and distortion. For instance, in a remote viewing experiment, a subject might accurately pick up the impression of, say, the Louisiana Superdome stadium, which is a huge, circular, silvery building with metal sides and a white dome that gleams in the sun but, because of secondary elaboration, dismiss it as improbable or else report it inaccurately as "a space ship in the middle of a city."[6] Ingo Swann's caution is borne out: the very act of labeling (which, after all, is a combination of verbalizing, analyzing, and categorizing) will distort the data.

Several people in my study also spoke at length about the need to leave the information uncontaminated by analysis and interpretation *as it is showing up.* Kathlyn Rhea, for instance, a much-sought-after San Francisco intuitive who works a lot with police detectives, health professionals, and psychotherapists, says that in recent years the various initial bits of psi information usually come into her brain immediately. (She nonetheless spends hours and sometimes days working with a detective or physician to put the various pieces together with their information in a logical, left-brained way.) Earlier in her career, she told me, "I had to learn to quit letting my conscious mind take over. I had to keep going back to the original information." Premature analysis can distort the truth.

Anne Armstrong, in reporting her impressions, does an impeccable job of simply stating what she sees even when it makes absolutely no sense to her, which is often the case, at least at the outset. She displays a kind of absolute trust in the information and in the process, and she follows it wherever it takes her, fragment by fragment, until something coherent takes shape.

She talks aloud the whole time she is receiving impressions, offering scrupulously unembellished descriptions of her impressions—no more, no less—so we get to come along with her and uncover the meaning of the information slowly, as it unfolds. It is this powerful combination of her reporting only the raw data of her initial impressions plus her rather freewheeling, spontaneous willingness to follow it wherever it leads her that keeps her information so free of distortion.[7]

One very psychic woman, a high-level school administrator with a strong, cognitive grip on things, is very clear and accurate with total strangers but declines to do readings for friends or family (except in emergencies) because she has such a hard time taking her "cognitive self" out of it. She says this is because she tends to analyze and rework and knead the data to fit what she already knows about them or what she wishes for them. For this reason, it is much easier for her to work with strangers, where she is happily ignorant and disinterested. This is also why most people, regardless of their skill levels, have difficulty getting accurate information about themselves on a consistent basis.

I've noticed in my own practice that I am now much less impeded by secondary elaboration than I used to be. With continued experience and careful tracking of my hits and misses, a natural pattern emerged, and I began to trust the information that I was getting, exactly as it was.

An early example of a useful psi fragment is the time I was listening to a rather tired and beaten-down middle-aged man, a man who felt entitled to nothing. He was struggling with an oppressive sense of entrapment, both in his marriage and in his work in the family business, and he was telling me about how fearful he was of making changes in his life. As he spoke, I would occasionally glimpse flashes of a very faint but fetching image of a young boy about eight or nine, romping in the snow with two big dogs.

The flashes of feeling accompanying the image were wonderful—full of freedom, joy, expansiveness, unselfconscious spontaneity, and boundless energy.

We had reached several dead ends anyway, so, with nothing much to lose, I asked him a simple question about whether he could ever remember a time when he felt carefree and joyful and strong. He thought for a while and then started to tell me about his favorite times as a boy on his grandparents' farm. This was a place his family used to visit every Christmas. Somehow at the farm, with this set of grandparents, he was able to get free of the constrictive demands of his everyday life. And, yes, there were two golden retrievers he adored, and he would take them into the field by the woods in back of the house to roll around and wrestle with them in the snow.

As he spoke about those days, he reconnected with his old love for physical activity, his enjoyment of the outdoors, his comfort with his own body, and the carefree exuberance he had felt then. I watched, delighted, as he literally transformed before my very eyes, looking and sounding like an altogether different man—younger, happier, more energized, and even sexier. This childhood memory became key to helping him get back in touch with his courage, hope, and energy, all of which he'd be needing if he was going to make the necessary changes in his life.

Nowadays, images like the one with the boy and the dogs come to me regularly as I work in my office. As clients speak of their lives, insights and images spontaneously appear, sometimes soft, fleeting, and hazy, and at other times quite sharp and clear. For me, the trick is to always be alert to them and to hold them in my awareness, but lightly, giving them room to move or change in any direction they want to. By neither dismissing them out of hand nor pouncing on them and nailing them down too quickly, I can make the most of these wonderful glimmers.

So another feature of gaining access to psi is giving attention to the most fleeting of impressions and being willing to leave them alone, undistorted by the analytic workings of the left side of the brain.

ENERGETIC AMPLIFICATION

The most difficult component to put into words—initially it is hard for many of us to perceive, let alone describe—is the subtle expansion and movement of electromagnetic energy that occurs in and around the body just before and during these appearances of psi. Although subtle and hard to describe, this shift in energy is probably what lies at the bottom of the appearance of psi. My explanation of how and why I think this is so appears in the chapter that follows, where I explain the physics of ESP. But for now, let me just try to describe the phenomenon in my own and in other people's words.

The kind of energy I'm talking about here has been called many things: chi, prana, biophysical energy, electromagnetic energy, orgone, vital life force, and many more. At the subatomic level, it is the stuff we are all made of and what we all come from. It flows through and around the body in loops and lines,[8] entering and exiting via hundreds of large and small energy vortices (usually referred to as chakras).

When we see the aura, what we are looking at is the denser part of this energy field, the part immediately around the body, which is "thicker" and therefore more visible. (Our fields actually extend way beyond us—in fact, they extend infinitely—and they permeate the body as well.)

In a healthy body, the energy field is ample, coherent, dynamic, and complex, playing host to many variable frequencies. Less healthy fields are punier, more rigid, and more constricted and hold fewer frequencies. When we've just had a jog, when we feel happy or loving, or when we've just meditated or gotten a massage or listened to a gorgeous piece of music, our fields get bigger and fluffier, as they do also when we've been hanging out in a very energized crowd at a church, a concert, or a stadium or have just spent time by the ocean or running water.[9]

In fact, illness and health probably show up in the field first and then work their way down into the denser, more rigidly organized aspects of the body's actual tissue. For our purposes here, let me just say that the fact that we need a big, fluffy, complex field for both good health and for strong psi reception underlines the importance of taking good care of the body while heightening psi activity. I'll be saying lots more about this later on.

Although energy fields are subtle and initially hard to perceive, anyone can learn to sense their own and, even more readily, those of other people. With a little attention, training, and practice, you begin to feel a thick, almost gummy quality in the air around the body. In the body itself, energy feels like a very subtle, electrical, buzzy, vibratory internal sensation. With continued focus and attention, these energies become more and more palpable and manipulable. Not surprisingly, body workers, energy healers, yoga practitioners, and meditators are usually highly attuned to it.

As with every other autonomic or unconscious function, the more we can perceive and note such phenomena while they are occurring, the more we can heighten and direct their effects. We can make things happen when we want them to, not by dint of hard-driving, proactive effort, but just by imagining the sight, sound, and feel of their appearance. Phoenix intuitive trainer Victor R. Beasley, Ph.D., puts it very succinctly: "We're all hardwired for this, so when we focus on it, it expands. Energy will always follow thought." And energy will follow imagery even more readily.[10]

Before discussing these "amped-up" energies, however, I want to mention that a very high percentage of the people in my study seemed to carry around an inordinate supply of baseline energy to start with. In fact, at certain times in their lives, several of them experienced trouble with their electrical appliances—odd malfunctionings, such as hair dryers fizzling out at a touch, toasters burning out, and lightbulbs popping out whenever they passed by. (Even more fantastic, three people independently told me that on occasion a whole string of street lamps would go out while they were driving under them.)

One woman told me with some chagrin that years ago, after a couple of months in her new apartment, her landlord announced that she would either have to start replacing her own lightbulbs or else pay more rent, because she had gone through so many of them quickly. And a substantial number of subjects reported that watches wouldn't work properly for them.[11]

These phenomena seemed more likely to occur when the person was in a highly charged emotional state, usually upset or angry, or else was entering a new stage of expanded psychic awareness. Several had taught themselves to center and calm themselves just before turning on the toaster or booting up the laptop during such periods of change.[12] All of this provides strong support for the idea that heightened electromagnetic energy is part and parcel of the psi experience.

Early psi researchers paid little attention to energy per se, but some of the researchers into psychokinesis, or PK, did look at variations in a subject's amplitude of energy and their resultant ability to direct it toward influencing physical objects. (Spoon bending, table tipping, intentional prayer, and healing can be included under PK.)

Malibu physiologist Dr. Valerie Hunt, a pioneer researcher in the study of the human energy field, has devised a system for measuring the electromagnetic amplitudes and frequencies of energy as it shifts in different people, especially high-energy psychics and healers. She validated what intuitives have been saying for a very long time: that there are specific, high frequencies associated with moving into psi territory, and that a strong, psi-generating field is always characterized by its amplitude and complexity—in other words, a full range of frequencies, and lots of them.[13]

So it's safe to say that there is a shift into a heightened energy state as people launch into receiving psi information. Sometimes this can be felt as a warmth or tingling, a delicate kind of vibration, or as a subtle but positive feeling of humming peacefulness, a mellow kind of "high." But I confess, even the most articulate people struggled to find words to properly describe this experience. And each person tended to have his or her own characteristic, unique set of sensations and responses.

For many, this involved powerful sensations around the back, top, and front of the head. For instance, Vivian Bochenek described a feeling of her head opening, as if the sutures across the top of her skull were actually moving, along with a sense of energy running faster, up and down through her body, and a feeling of expanding and moving outside of herself. She told me, "It's like the only thing that's holding you is the texture of your skin . . . but you aren't just in the vessel. . . . You've become movement and flow. . . . Your body is here, but you are everywhere."

Bryan Christopher told me, "My surroundings disappear. It all becomes energy and starts to move. I become part of that, part of the movement."

Emilie Conrad-Da'oud described it as "like being in a state of molecular refinement, as if I'm resonating with a whole molecular infrastructure that has no boundaries." (Try to keep descriptions like these in mind when you're reading about the physics of ESP in the next chapter.)

Professional intuitive and writer Alan Vaughan told me he experiences a tingling in his forehead, energy arousal in his solar plexus, and tingles all over, running up and down his back, "kind of like a rush."

Similarly, intuitive counselor and healer Sue Greer describes feeling a kind of simultaneous softening and heightening of energy inside of her. Sometimes, she says, "There's something like an adrenalin rush, a hyperalertness, a heightening, along with a softening at the same time."

I love Laura Chapman's description. She says the feeling is similar to "standing chi kung, open attention with a full, connected flow of energy all through the body." She says she knows she is speaking the truth when she experiences "a shimmer up the spine, an energy rush, followed by a line of energy that goes down into the ground, like a pole of energy that moves through the hips and legs, anchoring down into the ground, like a great big YES."[14]

Other descriptions of these energetic shifts include: a warming sensation; tingling; waves or flutterings of energy; a sense of lightness or weightlessness; a warmth or tingling coming in from the right or, less frequently, from the left; a sense of disappearing boundaries; a feeling of expansion, heightening, or softening; a dissolving physically into energy; waves of warmth or color coming from around the heart; seeing colors (silvers, violets, and blues seem to predominate with my inter-viewees); and hearing tones or high-pitched sounds.[15] Often these shifts are accompanied by feelings of elation, joy, peace-fulness, love, inclusion, completion, wholeness, and a sense that everything is exactly as it should be.

For me, too, this energetic shift is a palpable thing. As the psychic information is coming through, I feel an expansion, a sense of extension beyond my skin, and a tingling, buzzy height-ening of my awareness. Along with a greater acuteness in my perception, I feel softer, mellower, and much more at peace. Al-though I feel great empathy during these times—more than usual, in fact—the feelings seem to pass right through me rather than soak into my cells and stay there the way they used to. I used to go home heavy and waterlogged with other people's pain; that happens less frequently nowadays.

It is this energetic aspect, I believe, that accounts for the fact that although I do much less proactive "work" in this psi-receptive state, more work actually gets done. Paradoxically, my clients reach their goals quickly, even though very little effort has been expended on my part, with far less of the dragging, pushing, prodding, persuading, and confronting that I used to do earlier in my career.

I think this is because when I'm working in this way, *it's not just me doing the work.* I'm part of a whole *field,* and assistance is everywhere. Subtle tools can exert great force when working in this way, at this energetic level.

You may have noticed by now that people's various descrip-tions of their experience of shifting, heightening energy call to mind some of the ways that metabolic and temporal lobe changes were described in chapter 2. Clearly, all of these factors work simultaneously to allow psi to come through. While modu-lations in the endocrine system[16] and shifts in brain functioning represent the *mechanics* of how the physical body negotiates its stretch to accommodate the heightened energies of psi, *the underlying feature of the psychic experience is the movement of the energy itself.*[17] I'll explain what I mean by this in the next chapter, including how feelings of love and gratitude can mobilize that movement of energy.

Explaining It

FIVE

The Physics of ESP, Love, and Imagery

This is the section I've been promising that explains the physics of psi and how and why the imagery that generates feelings of love and gratitude can activate our psychic process.[1]

I take the long way around, starting with the psychology of how we expand our boundaries beyond ourselves when we feel love and moving rather quickly into some pretty abstract but all-encompassing physics concepts. I wind up reporting on some exciting research that shows how the emotions of love and gratitude can actually change the frequencies and coherence of measurable oscillations in the body.

It's not easy material, but it's not impossible, either. And it's a very rewarding and exciting view of the universe, so try to stay with it. I restate the most abstract ideas several times, just because I myself found it helpful to keep hearing them. They took a while to sink in, but once they did, they explained a lot to me—everything, in fact.

As you read this, try to keep in mind all the ways that energy was described on earlier pages and how the various experiences of receiving psi were reported by the intuitives I interviewed. It's all here.

And finally, if physics just isn't your cup of tea and you feel your eyes glazing over, just skip ahead to chapter 6. These concepts show up in the imagery there, and you can absorb them with the right side of your brain through the exercises.

THE BOUNDARIES OF THE EGO

Psychology, in its earliest characterizations of human motivation and behavior, was pretty simplistic and reductionistic.[2] Freud's psychoanalysis portrayed human nature as motivated strictly by the need to alleviate the discomfort generated by our primitive, internal drives. In a similar vein, behaviorism, an outgrowth of early learning theory, described us as driven by the need to receive rewards and avoid punishment. The ego had a rather low-level job that was, quite literally, *self-serving*—it was there to maintain the individual self and negotiate between internal drives and external conditions.

These systems, not surprisingly, needed to perform some tricky intellectual footwork in order to explain altruistic behavior. When someone acted against apparent self-interest for the benefit of someone or something else, and even appeared *happy* about it, psychoanalysis and behaviorism were hard-pressed to find a reasonable explanation. Instances such as a parent gladly engaging in mind-numbing factory work so that a child could go to college or a stranger jumping into freezing water to save a drowning man's life or a soldier vying to be chosen for a suicide mission so he could die for his country during wartime were puzzlements. These examples were clearly more than just the expression of a masochistic character structure or the product of a person's intensely self-sacrificing conditioning.

In time, more sophisticated psychologies evolved that were able to reconcile the altruism issue by seeing the ego as having *movable boundaries.* The ego's executive decision to volunteer for the suicide mission, for instance, could still be seen as "self-serving" if the definition of *self* were enlarged. If the soldier's boundaries of self had expanded to include the whole country he was fighting for, then in this new, expanded identity, he was still acting in his own best interest. Psychologically and emotionally, he had, in effect, *become* his country.

Similarly, sacrificing parents and devoted lovers weren't demonstrating their pathological masochism; they had simply opened up their ego boundaries to include their loved ones so that they, too, were acting in their own best interest. The emotion of love had expanded the sense of self.

I confess, the old, cynical psychological reductionism that portrayed us all as selfish little piggies never made much sense to me. And though this new way of looking at the self may seem somewhat slick, I don't believe that it's just a convenient bit of sophistry, designed to keep psychoanalysis and behaviorism in business. Later developments in ego psychology and Jungian psychology affirm these expanded notions about what the self is. And certainly, ideas about our expanding and contracting boundaries are pervasive in every culture and are central to religious traditions the world over. They are also well supported by the exciting new ideas found in theoretical physics, which start to sound suspiciously like religion.

Because if we take a serious look at this notion of expanding and contracting boundaries, even our concrete, physical ones, from the point of view of these new scientific paradigms, we find that we are far less bound by our skins and our "selves" than we think. We aren't nearly as solid and contained as we appear. Matter is not solid; at the subatomic level, it is a collection of particles and waves. And when we examine the particles even more closely, we find that they aren't particles at all—they're actually little wave packets. When all is said and done, we're nothing but a lot of vibrating empty space.

What we think is solid stuff isn't—things aren't things, in fact. If you can get your mind around this, you can move to the next idea, that things are really *events*—events that emerge out of a vast, shifting and changing sea of *probable events*. But before I get too far into this, let me back up a bit and try to explain the main features of this new physics universe we live in.

It's no secret where I'm headed here, but let me state it anyway: if our "outer limits" aren't really our skins, then we can look at the occurrence of psi as a normal, plausible event. With expandable, permeable boundaries, our own and others', we can pick up all sorts of information from the outside world—about other people, places, and events—because, in a sense, even if it's only for a matter of nanoseconds, we would have *become* them. Through a momentary shift in our emotions and attitudes, the outside becomes inside and the inside outside. We have the ability to dissolve our fixed boundaries and expand into and merge with those things that we normally see as *other* by deliberately generating feelings of love, gratitude, and universal oneness.

THE BOUNDARIES OF MATTER

The brilliant work of David Bohm and several other modern theoretical physicists offers a framework to explain this intriguing view of reality. His system reconciles relativity theory and quantum theory and is becoming more and more widely accepted and developed the world over. It describes how we are, at the most basic levels, unrestricted, *nonlocal* beings, in spite of our current primitive, concrete ideas about space and distance. It tells us that time can only be something that happens in the *present* and how, in spite of our artificial constructs of past and future, we are really beings who live in a lot of parallel, concurrent *nows*.

Majestic and awe inspiring in its scope, Bohm's material overlaps beautifully with the enlightened awarenesses of mystical traditions the world over, from the beginning of time to the present (notwithstanding the fact that time *has* no beginning and "the past" is actually *concurrent* with now, as we will soon see). His work is destined to become the fundamental scientific paradigm to dominate the first half of the twenty-first century. And we couldn't be welcomed into the new millennium by a more gracious and soul-expanding set of ideas.

Bohm's central thesis is that the world and everything in it is a vast ocean of energy. What we perceive as separate parts— you, me, the chair, the dog, the trees, the air we breathe, the atmosphere surrounding the planet, and the stars in the next galaxy—are all part of a seamless whole (the *holomovement*) that is pulsing with life and intelligence. He calls this ocean of living energy the *implicate order* because it cannot be seen (or measured, except mathematically), only inferred.

Organizing this high-energy pool into various structures is the *superimplicate order,* a superinformation field that surrounds, interpenetrates, and underlies the implicate order, directing its unfolding into the relatively stable forms we perceive with our everyday senses—the *stuff* of the world as we know it (the *explicate order*).

In this sea of pure energy, there are no particles, no space or time. Space and time are properties of the three-dimensional world of the explicate order. (By the rules of quantum mechanics, space and time cannot exist without someone there to measure them.) But even our limited, three-dimensional version of reality, since it springs from the implicate order, has enfolded within it this vast, multidimensional consciousness. We and everything around us are made up of this energy, which, in a subtle but very real sense, is *conscious and alive.* Even a so-called vacuum, which is supposed to be nothing at all, is filled with it. In Bohm's world, there is no such thing as a true vacuum.

The energy of the implicate order is *pure movement.* It is *vibration, loaded with potential* for manifesting itself in an infinite array of forms. In other words, it's *probability in motion.* These probabilities are all co-present, existing alongside whatever "reality" has been manifested in the explicate order.

Interpenetrating and directing this energy is the *pure information* of the superimplicate order and, in turn, interpenetrating and directing that, a *supersuperimplicate order,* and so on, ad infinitum, each reality possessing subtler and subtler and deeper and deeper levels of intelligence. (Normally, we would say "higher and higher" levels of intelligence, but this would erroneously convey the idea of hierarchy, which cannot exist in the context of this multidimensional world. Hierarchy can happen only in a three-dimensional reality. In fact, the word *level* has a similar problem and is really a misnomer. The idea of a spectrum is a little better, if you can imagine an infinite spectrum of orders within orders that go from the most subtle varieties—pure light—to the most dense—matter.)

Our visible, palpable three-dimensional world (the explicate order) is derived from this multidimensional reality, in the same way that a little wave will form for a moment upon the surface of the ocean. (We might have originated from a primordial chemical soup, but before chemical soup, there was energy soup.)[3] And since all matter springs from this living, intelligent ocean of energy, all of it, too, is alive. *Everything in our world consists of this teeming, vibrating system of conscious energy, all around, between, and through everything.*

And each separate *thing* in the manifest world is *aware,* at this profound level of subtlety, of the overall plan in which it participates, infused as it is with the pulsating intelligence of the superimplicate order. Everything that exists or happens in the world, regardless of how random or chaotic it may appear, holds consciousness and reveals the pattern of the superorder in which it is embedded.

Even a rock is perceived as being alive in this system—not self-aware, the way human beings are—but with its own inclinations and tendencies. A rock would have a very dense kind of consciousness.

And enfolded within a rock's very dense consciousness— just as it is within yours and mine—would be everything in the universe, all of it co-present and from all time, past, present, and future. In fact, all the properties of this sea of energy are enfolded within each and every element of our everyday world, *regularly projecting into them in a pulsating manner.* The rock is actually not a collection of solid particles but an assembly of pulsating *events* that last for an instant and then fade away. It is as if a trillion trillion fireflies were all flashing at hyperspeed in its space, at a rate too fast for our biological systems to track, and thus making the rock appear solid to us.

This pulsating activity both focuses and disperses information. Information comes from the superimplicate and implicate order into the rock and travels from the rock back out again into the holomovement in an automatic, coherent feedback system. Each incoming wave brings information from all points in space, while each outgoing wave spreads information to all points in space.

And since the implicate order is nonlocal, similar forms resonate and are connected to one another regardless of their location in three-dimensional space and time.[4] Thus similar kinds of rocks *influence* one another in their rocklike way and are connected in their *rock-intelligence,* as it were. In fact, if we were to take a closer look at the rock, this time from the subtler and deeper aspect of the superimplicate order (which is enfolded into the implicate order and thus into the rock), we would find that even the dense consciousness of the rock pulsates with omniscient energy.

Another way to put this is to say that every point in the implicate order is perfectly interpenetrated by every other. And any given moment in the implicate order has the whole of time and space enfolded within it. There is no cause and effect here, because there are no time sequences; *nothing really happens—it just is.* The implicate order's central quality of *nonlocality* pulses into our everyday world, and, to most physicists, nonlocality means instantaneous communication.

To summarize and restate, we inhabit a universe that is a seamless, coherent whole. The separation of objects is an attribute of the explicit order, as are space and time. We actually inhabit a universe where every point is interpenetrated by every other point.

This universe is made up of the implicate order, a vast ocean of living, conscious, intelligent energy underlying, surrounding, overlaying, and interpenetrating the ordinary world of our experience. And embedded in this implicate order is the superimplicate order, a vast—in fact infinite—information field, a protointelligence organizing and directing the energy of the implicate order and enfolded within it. From the implicate and superimplicate orders (of which there are an infinite number in an infinite array or spectrum) is derived the manifest world of our experience.

This world appears solid and three-dimensional, but, because it is born of the implicate and superimplicate orders, it really pulsates with intelligence that is nonlocal—everywhere at once—and that holds all of time in a co-present fashion. Since hierarchies, structures, and grids—not to mention years, days, and minutes—don't exist at this level of subtlety, things just *are,* embedded within one another, with all past and future events happening now.

Similar things pulsate in a similar way and instantaneously communicate with and influence one another at these subtle levels through a kind of synchronized resonation. And as these like things resonate, together they pulse their influence back to the implicate order, helping to reshape and reform the holomovement in a coherent, seamlessly holistic way. The feedback loop is continuous, the rocks pulsating their consciousness into the implicate order and the implicate order pulsating its intelligence back into the rocks. In the words of computer scientist Douglas Hofstadter, "It turns out that an eerie type of chaos can lurk just behind a facade of order—and yet, deep inside the chaos lurks an even eerier type of order."[5]

Again, because everything is enfolded within everything else, this vast information field is everywhere, inside of us and outside of us. It coexists with and pulses in our ordinary reality. Because of its qualities of nonlocality, information from all time is co-present and available in its entirety. Past and future are artificial, arbitrary constructs that occur only in the concrete world of watches and calendars, not at this subtle level of reality.

No doubt by now you have noticed that this description of an infinite sea of intelligent energy with the properties of ubiquity, infinity, and omniscience sounds an awful lot like anybody's basic description of God. Add Bohm's notion that there is intelligence and order behind all the myriad appearances of chaos and randomness in our manifest world. Finally, toss in his bottom-line idea that we are all made of the same stuff— each one of us containing in each particle of us (which really isn't a particle anyway, but a vibration in space, intersecting with a probability) every other one of us, and indeed every co-present, nonlocal thing in the universe, everything that ever was, is, or will be. If we include this idea of our all being one, part of a vast and seamless resonating whole, then, it seems to me, we've got the essence of any religion worth its rituals and liturgies.

Of course, in this paradigm, the specific differences in religious doctrines and formats will show up at the denser, shallower, and less subtle ends of the consciousness spectrum, but at the lighter, deeper, and subtler ends, these dogmas divest themselves of their distinctions and dissolve into one another. This reminds me of the way that some people report their near-death experiences. First they see the specific gods and religious icons of their upbringing and cultural training, but then, the deeper and farther down the tunnel and into the experience they travel, the closer they get to an undifferentiated white light of ineffable warmth, love, peace, and joy. Not surprisingly, in Bohm's physics, the subtlest level of energy is in fact pure light.

Most of us have had a direct *experience* of God, but when called upon to try and describe or explain it, unless we are poets or abstract artists, we find it a daunting task indeed, hampered as we are by the sorry inadequacy of language and linear thinking. But I think Bohm has pulled it off.

Certainly most of us have reached adulthood concluding that, as one of my friends recently said to me with some conviction, "I do know this much: God is *not* an old guy with a beard." I'm pretty clear on that myself but have always had trouble articulating a sufficiently expansive, encompassing alternative vision. This new scientific paradigm, the robust child of a passionate marriage between physics and mathematics, is probably about as close as I'm likely to get to wrapping my mind around the idea of a godhead.

BENTOV'S PENDULUM

But even if we accept Bohm's ideas as a reasonable description of the nature of the universe and believe that we are suffused with and surrounded by a conscious, living, pulsing, intelligent energy, an awesome protointelligence of infinite and nonlocal capability, it still doesn't answer the question of how we are able to consciously hook up to it and gather information from it. Bohm gives us some clues when he talks about intelligence pulsing in and out of matter and when he discusses the idea of like consciousnesses *resonating* with one another.

But it was Itzhak Bentov who put this part of the puzzle together for me, even though he died in a plane crash long before he was able to develop his ideas further or to take advantage of our current discoveries in these matters. A humorous, unpretentious, brilliant theoretician and inventor, he was a natural teacher and popularizer of complex ideas, and he spelled them out clearly in his remarkable little book, *Stalking the Wild Pendulum: On the Mechanics of Consciousness,* first published in 1977 and reprinted by his widow in 1988. Surprisingly, very little of his thinking is outdated. His book is one I continually refer to, and my beloved copy is a dog-eared, margin-scribbled, well-worn old mess.

Bentov, like Bohm, talks about the fact that all apparently solid matter is nothing but vibration, and he explains how particles turn out to be nothing but "wave packets." In fact, he tells us, our human bodies oscillate up and down at a rate of about seven times per second but in ways that are too speedy and too minuscule for us to perceive with our limited, lumbering senses.

These vibrations or oscillations, when broken down, possess the same characteristics as the motion of a pendulum. In fact, everything in the universe moves in the way that a pendulum does, whether it pulsates concentrically, moves back and forth, travels in an orbit, or turns about itself. The pendulum movement applies to everything that is. And it has a fascinating dynamic built into it, just by its very nature.

We know from watching a grandfather clock that a pendulum is a system that always appears to reach two points of rest: one still point happens when it has traveled in one direction as far as it can and arrives at the place where it is about to reverse direction, and the other still point is the stopping of its movement on the other side, before again reversing direction.

Here is Bentov's awesome conceptual clincher: pendulums have some remarkable features at their still points, *as does anything that is at absolute rest.* Between the time a pendulum has come to a full stop and the point at which it starts on its return trip, it traverses a zero-point, where *all bets are off regarding the causal relationship between time and space.* At those two still points, the pendulum becomes, for a very short period of time, *nonmaterial,* and expands into space at infinite velocity. Thanks to relativity theory, this is a mathematical certainty.

Another way to say this is that in a state of rest, an oscillator tunnels into a spacelike dimension where, at infinite velocities, it becomes omnipresent. Then, when it returns to its state of motion, it reenters the world of three dimensions and continues with business as usual.

Our body is the pendulum. It oscillates up and down at a rate of about seven cycles per second[6] and therefore reaches a state of rest at the rate of fourteen times a second. This means that fourteen times every second (and probably a lot more, but at least that), we are expanding at a very high speed through subjective time into objective space. In no time at all, we come back again, but during that "no-time," we have been out into other dimensions and realities, dispensing and collecting information. This is just as Bohm described the continuous pulsing of protointelligence, between the implicate and explicate orders. Bentov simply offers us the mechanics of the pendulum to show us how this can actually operate in our three-dimensional world.

Sometimes, under certain circumstances, we are capable of bringing the data back into our three-dimensional world—if we're wired sensitively or if we've trained our minds to do so. Both Bohm and Bentov felt that meditation was the best way to train the mind to spend longer periods of subjective time out there in space-time during those blinks away. This is because meditation lowers the frequencies of our brain waves and, in so doing, *expands the perceived time that we are "out."*

In the meantime, our solid physical reality goes on as usual, except for these little "pauses" when we take off and come back. Most of us live our lives unaware of this dynamic, and, although we might consciously experience a few spontaneous bleedthroughs from these "trips" of ours, they usually remain an unexplained anomaly to us. Frequently, for want of anything better to do, we assign magical powers to these occurrences.

But, in fact, we are always *blinking on and off*; we are coming and going all the time.

Here, then, is the dynamic—the three-dimensional mechanics, if you will—that explains how Bohm's holomovement and the enfolded layers of the implicate order can pulse their intelligence into us, and how we pulse our feedback back into it, in a seamless, holistic dance of co-creation.

Now, although the body as a whole is an oscillator that vibrates at the measurable rate of 7 Hz (cycles per second), our atoms vibrate at a much faster rate: 10^{15} Hz, in fact, a frequency far too fast to measure. We can assume, however, that in our normal, waking consciousness, our atoms are blinking on and off at different times, in an unsynchronized fashion, so that parts of us are appearing and parts of us disappearing all the time. In other words, we are partially "out" all the time.

Bentov wrote in his arch but gentle way, "In the unlikely event that total coherency occurs in the body (this may occur at very high levels of consciousness), then, naturally, the whole body will blink off and on as a unit, and we may expect to see some very unusual things occurring." Mostly, he limited himself to looking at the 7 Hz rate for the body as a whole, because it was one that could be measured in the three-dimensional world.

However, he felt it highly likely that meditation, which heightens and coheres consciousness, could be used to help the body get closer to this state of synchronized oscillation and thus extend the power and range of our subjective length of stay in the "out" zone. If large parts of us are blinking on and off in unison, big chunks of us would be at the still point simultaneously, and our awareness and recall of our omniscient reach into infinity would be far greater.[7]

Similarly, if our blinking on and off were synchronized with that of others, we could meet them and possibly even interact with them during those short periods of time "out." In a sense, all of creation would be in constant and instantaneous communication on the level of this spacelike universe, with some of us more aware of this than others. And those of us on the same wavelength (literally) would be in close contact indeed. Put another way, people attuned to the same frequency would be resonating all the time and communicating easily in the "out" zone. This is why, Bentov posits, it is commonplace for the same idea or invention to pop up in several locations simultaneously around the globe.

Bohm and Bentov's notion that meditation creates a more synchronized, harmonious, and coherent pattern of oscillations within the body is supported both by verbal descriptions of the internal experience of meditating and by research. Indeed, all but two of my forty-three psychic subjects professed to meditate on a regular basis. And "meditation" was the most frequently stated and first-offered answer to the question "Do you engage in any purposeful practice to cultivate this [psychic] ability?"

The Institute of HeartMath, a nonprofit research and training organization in Boulder Creek, California, has done some interesting research that appears to support this idea.[8] The institute has developed a kind of heart-based meditation technique, which their studies show can smooth out subjects' heart rate variability and entrain brain wave frequencies to match the more balanced, even heart rhythms.

It is their contention that when the electrical patterns of the brain synchronize with the far more powerful electrical rhythms of the heart, a kind of harmonious coherence is achieved among heart, brain, and the entire body. This, they claim, greatly increases intuitive awareness. In the words of the institute's founder, Doc Lew Childre, this kind of meditation "builds a *standing wave of coherence* [emphasis added] between your heart, brain and body. This same wave of coherence also unites spirit, emotions and mind. The resulting intuitive awareness further penetrates into the . . . domain which exists beyond time and space." In this state of internal coherence and "amplified peace," "*blocks of intuitive information can come to you in seconds* [emphasis added]."[9]

This entrainment occurs when frequencies lock among heart rhythms, respiration, pulse transit time (a measure of blood pressure), and brain waves. According to research director Rollin McCraty, this synchronization causes brain wave patterns to slow down to frequencies of around .1 Hz and below.[10] It is here, he says, at these very low frequencies, that great power resides for healing, perceptual shifts, experience reprocessing, and intuiting.

This bears out Bentov's hypothetical idea from 1977 that if we could somehow manage to synchronize the varying oscillations from the different parts of our bodies (which he, too, thought could be attained through meditation), we would achieve some coherence in our bodies' rhythmic cycles of blinking on and off. The still points would then hold far more subjective time, and so greater amounts of universal information could be gleaned, gathered, and brought back with recall. In other words, we would be more psychic and intuitive. These studies appear to have demonstrated, at least partially, Bentov's hypothetical situation and successfully measured the effects on oscillations throughout the body. I should mention, however, that their reports of heightened intuition are at this time strictly anecdotal.[11]

At the Institute of HeartMath, the meditation process focuses on the heart. People are taught to direct their attention to their hearts and to deliberately and consciously generate and hold feelings of love, care, compassion, or appreciation there for several minutes. This is what produces the entrainment of heart and brain.

As the focus continues and the state deepens, the frequencies flatten out even further, to below .1 Hz. The heart frequency then drives the entire system, entraining the nonlinear biological oscillators in the brain stem, intestines, vascular system, and other areas to follow suit in one coherent internal rhythm pattern of low-frequency, amplified peace. Heartfelt emotions of love and gratitude are what fuel this powerful engine.

Guided imagery, at least the way I define it, is in fact the meditative tool used in these experiments to produce this heart-focused state. Initially, imagery is what is called upon to deliberately generate these loving feelings. Later, with practice, the simple *memory of the feeling itself* does the trick.

The sequence in these experiments goes something like this: subjects are first coached to imagine they are breathing through their hearts, a form of kinesthetic imagery that keeps the focus heart centered. Then they are encouraged to remember times when they felt loving, felt loved, or experienced heartfelt sentiment for someone or something, a practice that I call simple, *feeling-state* imagery. If they are upset, they are coached to imagine they are holding the upset in their hearts and then stirring the feelings and homogenizing them, as if with a whisk or blender, to disperse them. This is *metaphoric* imagery.

Once this heart-based imagery is an established, familiar routine, the feeling can be called up almost instantaneously. Most of the time, a lot of preliminary imagery is no longer necessary, except at times of unusual emotional stress.

So now we have come full circle, from the psychological notion that a loving heart can expand the boundaries of the ego, to the ideas of David Bohm and theoretical physics that we live in a universe with no boundaries, dwelling in a sea of seamless, vibrating energy, alive and pulsing with omniscient, nonlocal, and infinite intelligence, to Bentov's suggestion that our bodies are oscillators and that when they are internally and externally synchronized into a coherent, resonating system, they can consciously connect with large chunks of this universal intelligence, to the research findings that meditation is a powerful tool for consciously achieving this coherence and that one of the most powerful forms of meditation is imagery that generates a loving heart.

Bentov, like many others, writes of how evolution is developing and refining the human nervous system, taking the heart and brain closer and closer to a quality of consciousness that approaches "the absolute," a point in frequency that is high enough to resonate with the highest levels of creation. As we develop in this way, he tells us, we will naturally and simultaneously grow in our "inner moral values and development of the heart. . . . [We] will automatically tend to help people in need, and will radiate an energy that on the physical level is expressed as the emotion called 'love.'"[12]

Bentov explains that he is not talking about romantic love here—processed in the body at second chakra level, the energy vortex located around three inches down from the navel. Instead, he is referring to something far more universal—heart chakra level, oscillating in the center of the chest. He says, "We would define love as energy and not an emotion, since emotions are confined to the physical and astral levels of reality. Beyond those levels emotions are not encountered. Therefore, what we call 'love' is an energy or radiation that pervades the whole cosmos." He adds in one of his breathtakingly brilliant, offhanded asides, "It is possibly the basis of what we know as the phenomenon of gravitation."[13]

One apparent inconsistency in the heart-imagery research had me puzzled for a while, and possibly it has you confused as well: if meditation and heart imagery *slow down* brain wave frequencies, how could this process allow us to hook up with the *higher* frequencies of the more subtle and evolved energy of the implicate order? Wouldn't we want to be generating higher frequencies in our brain waves, not lower ones, to match the subtle vibration of this sea of intelligence?

After a discussion with physicist Fred Alan Wolf[14] and psychologist Deborah Rozman, the answer became clear. As it turns out, I could have found it tucked away in Bentov's book, in a segment I'd been scooting past each time I'd read it.

Here it is: solid matter is made up of larger, slower waves or frequencies. The higher in consciousness we go (or as Bohm would say, the deeper and subtler we go into the implicate and superimplicate orders), the smaller and faster these frequencies become. At the highest (subtlest) level, what Bentov calls *the absolute*, the size of the waves is so minute and their frequency so high that they are invisible. The waves are so small and their crests and valleys (their points of rest) come so close to each other that they overlap and look like a flat line on a graph. In this way, a state of rest is reached, in which motion is just potential motion and the energy of the system becomes infinitely large. Movement and rest are fused into one. It all becomes a kind of humongous still point.

Meditation and heart-based imagery slow our brain waves down, creating a greater coherence in all the oscillating and blinking off and on that our systems are doing. This produces in us an expanded perception during our still points, the points of rest at which we expand out into all points in the universe at infinite speed. In this state of expanded subjective time, we can better absorb and bring back to our manifest world the information we collect out there. That is why taking our brain waves down into the lower ranges is so powerful and effective.

But the reason we can collect all that data in the first place is this: it is at our still points that we are matching *and resonating with* the so-high-as-to-be-still-point frequencies of the absolute intelligence of the superimplicate order. Our momentarily flat waves at our still points (super–high frequency, super–low amplitude) match the perfectly calm, still surface of the infinite sea of pure consciousness. And in this way, we blend with the highest frequencies in the universe. Although this is only the minutest of blinks in clock time, it traverses eternities in space-time.

PART 2

Activating and Using Your Psychic Ability

ψ

Imagery to
Access Psi

As you can see, we have a lot of information about the nature of psi experience—what it's about, how it works, what life experiences are likely to predispose us to it, and what actually happens in the moments just before and during a psychic opening, particularly the kind that comes by way of the open heart.

We've also seen that imagery can powerfully and easily reconstruct the core elements that set the stage and allow for psychic opening. It can encourage a consistent posture; it can relax, clear, and still the mind; it can create a special, sacred space around the imaginer; it can bolster belief and help set intention; and it is the perfect vehicle for opening and expanding the energy around the heart, which in turn creates coherent, systemwide oscillations in the body that extend the subjective time spent out in nonlocal space.

In addition to setting the stage for psychic opening, imagery can also replicate the conditions that allow the information to come through. By definition, it keeps us in receptive mode and turns our attention inward; its rich, sensory nature is able to seduce us gently out of strict, analytic mode so that our hearts can trust the information as it comes to us, unedited and as is; and imagery can be used to quickly amplify our easily influenced energetic fields. Imagery is simultaneously the natural by-product and the actual generator of altered state work and psi activity.

ψ ψ ψ

The imagery scripts that follow work best when they are read aloud to you so that you can just relax, listen, and follow the narrative. You may want to record them in your own voice or have someone else read them to you.

If you do decide to record the imagery yourself, you may want to experiment a bit in the beginning until you hit upon the words, phrasing, and pacing that most suits you. Leave pauses that are long enough to give your imagination the time it needs to get the job done; generally people tend to narrate a little too fast in the beginning.

The ellipses (...) indicate that a brief pause is in order. Spaces between paragraphs encourage longer pauses. And *(pause)* appears when an even longer interval is suggested. Of course, it's up to you to decide on the most compatible pacing for you.

Soothing, inspiring background music enhances the depth and intensity of imagery for most people, so experiment with different kinds of music to see what's most effective for you. However, if you are so sensitive to music or so inclined to analyze it (especially if you were a student of music or a professional musician) that its presence diverts you from the experience, you might be better off without it.

It's a good idea to try to use the same location to work with your imagery, someplace quiet, safe, comfortable, and where you know you won't be disturbed. Feel free to turn off the phone, lock the door, or even sit out in the car if that is your only refuge. Using the same place and the same music each time will help you create a quicker and deeper response to the imagery because of the immediate associations you will have made with these conditions.

Most people do better sitting up than lying down, simply because there's a tendency to fall asleep from the relaxation that the imagery encourages. If you find you have a problem staying awake, avoid soft lighting, keep your eyes partially open, and sit up, with your back a few inches away from the back of the chair. If you find that you are still nodding off, try listening while walking in a place that doesn't require you to pay a lot of attention to where you're going—perhaps a treadmill or a track.

Whether you are sitting, lying down, or walking, try to keep your head, neck, and spine straight. This helps keep your energy flowing and prevents you from collecting the muscular kinks that sometimes result from staying still for longer periods than you are accustomed to.

Believe it or not, imagery is more powerful in a group than alone, so you may want to collect a study group of like-minded people, a comfortable collection of friends or colleagues who are interested in developing their psi capabilities. This will allow you to take advantage of the collective resonating field that a whole group can generate. The altered state is contagious, and the group synergy that results from the interaction of all of those individual energy fields, jointly engaged in opening to psi, gives each member valuable extra mileage.[1]

Touch, too, is a powerful accompaniment to imagery, and for this heart-opening psi imagery, it's an especially good idea to work with one hand over your heart, palm down flat, over the center of the chest. Aside from reinforcing and deepening the effects of the heart-focused imagery,[2] touch, like consistent location and music, serves as a conditioning cue. Using these tools regularly, you can develop a simple but powerful shortcut for immediately gaining access to psi material.

Similarly, it's a good idea to use the same beginning sequence with each of your imagery exercises. I generally encourage deep, deliberate breathing as a way to start, which of course also elicits relaxation and a dropping down into the body. This, along with placing your hand over your heart and some standard beginning imagery—usually remembering a favorite time or place—promotes consistency and is one of the ways I like to begin. All these things become cues that accelerate the process of opening to psi, and they also combine to slow down the busy mind and body and prepare the way for deeper work.

Don't be surprised if you have some interesting body responses from practicing your imagery, especially in the beginning or each time you reach a new level of consciousness. Many people experience a change in body temperature, some getting warmer and others colder. Some people become light-headed or tingly around their scalp or hands and feet. Others experience little involuntary muscle jerks. Tears, runny noses, and a desire to cough or yawn are also commonplace. Often people think they've fallen asleep when actually they haven't, they've just been in a deep altered state. The tip-off is their ability to bring their awareness back immediately to the here and now when the imagery is over.

Keep a pen and notebook within easy reach so that you can jot down your notes about your experience once each exercise is over. Just as with your dreams, your memory of these imagery experiences will dissipate very quickly once you've made large-muscle movements, such as getting up and walking a few steps to get your notebook. So it's best to keep your writing materials close by.

Finally, always remember to be kind and respectful toward yourself as you engage in this process. No forcing, criticizing, demanding, or proactive orchestrating, please. Remember that the most nourishing ground for imagery is a gentle, soft, receptive state of mind. If you find yourself being too tense or demanding of yourself and can't seem to cut it out, put the exercise aside for a while and do something else. Then come back to it at a mellower time.

ψ ψ ψ

This first script is simple, heart-opening imagery, very basic but quite powerful. It becomes the launching pad for the more complex imagery that follows, but it also stands alone as a complete exercise by itself. You can use it not only to help you gain access to intuitive information, but also to settle yourself down when you're agitated. It will help you lower your blood pressure and enhance your immune system. Some people even use it before a difficult meeting, performance, or audition, because it replaces over-the-top anxiety with expansive, loving feelings.[3]

HEART-FOCUSING IMAGERY

(approximately 10 minutes)

To begin with, try to position yourself as comfortably as you can, shifting your weight until you can sense that your body is well supported . . . with your head, neck and spine straight . . .

And settling down into the center of your body . . . more and more, just dropping down into your body, with each deep, full, cleansing breath . . . inhaling as fully as you comfortably can . . . all the way down into the belly if you can . . . and breathing all the way out . . . fully and easily . . . (pause) . . .

And again, breathing deeply, all the way down into the belly . . . and maybe even feeling your abdomen rise, the way a child's does when it's sleeping . . . slowly and gently . . . and then releasing the breath with the exhale . . .

And this time, as you breathe in . . . sending the warm energy of the breath to any part of your body that's tense or sore or tight . . . and feeling it warm and loosen and soften all around and through the tension . . . and releasing it with the outbreath . . . so that more and more, you can feel your breath moving toward all the tight places . . . softening them . . . and breathing them out . . .

And noticing any distracting thoughts that might show up . . . and breathing those out, too . . . so that for just a moment, the mind is empty . . . for just a split second, it is free and clear and still . . .

And noticing in a friendly but detached way any emotions that might be coming up to the surface . . . and seeing that you can release those, too, with the outbreath . . . so that more and more, you can feel peaceful and quiet . . . steady and still . . . like a lake with no ripples . . .

And now, if you would, allowing yourself to focus your attention on your heart . . . and just putting your awareness there . . . curious about how it feels inside your heart . . . with all the gentle focus you can bring to bear . . . and perhaps even putting the flat palm of your hand over it . . .

And just keeping your awareness there . . . connecting to the gentle, powerful rhythms of your heart . . . sensing it pulsing all through your body . . .

And now beginning to breathe through your heart . . . sensing that the breath is actually coming in through your heart . . . (pause) . . . and breathing out through your heart . . . soft and warm and steady . . . in and out . . .

And you might even begin to feel a kind of warmth and fullness gathering all around and through your heart . . . very soft and nourishing . . . as you continue to focus your attention there . . . and breathe your breath there . . . right through the center of your heart . . .

(long pause)

And still attuned to the steady rhythm, in and out . . . you might bring your awareness to a time when you felt a lot of love and gratitude . . . maybe a memory that comes to mind . . .

Maybe a time when you were alone in nature, filled with the beauty all around you . . . maybe soaking in the generous warmth of the sunlight . . . or perhaps it was nighttime, under a vast, moonlit, star-filled sky . . . (pause) . . . or maybe it was a time when you were safely snuggled up, soft and warm and close, to someone very dear ... (pause) ... or perhaps you can re-member holding a baby, breathing in the scent of soft hair, and feeling velvety skin on your cheek ... (pause) ... it could be a time you romped with a special pet you loved ... (pause) ... or maybe it's your memory of sitting on the soft lap of a grand-mother, hearing her soft, low voice and taking in the scent of the soap on her skin ... (pause) ... or maybe it's a time you ran a triumphant race, enjoying the smooth and easy motion of your own body ... or it could be a time you communed with angels and celestial music ...

So you're just deliberately calling one of these times to mind ... and all the sights and sounds ... maybe hearing a voice ... catching a scent ... feeling a touch on your hand or cheek or brow ... or just remembering a certain quality in the air ... a warmth all through your body ... and you're just allowing yourself to be there again ... as you continue to breathe through the center of your heart ... feeling all the fullness, the richness, the power there ... and just letting it fill you ...

(long pause)

Allowing all the love and sweetness to fill your heart ... and overflow into the surrounding spaces of your body ... spilling over and filling your whole chest and torso ... warming and suffusing your back and your belly ... softly pulsing into every limb ... and up into your shoulders and neck ... so you're just letting the rich-ness of this feeling overflow your heart ... your whole body res-onating with the pulse of these powerful, loving feelings ...

Your whole body beating with one heart ... and even feeling the air around you begin to pulse with the steady power of this loving energy ... radiating outward ... creating a powerful field of pulsing energy all around and through you ... an expanding cushion of vibrant energy ... of dancing light and color ... as you continue to breathe it into your heart ... adding to the fullness there ... and breathe it out into the world ... adding to the rich-ness around you ...

(pause)

Residing in the loving seat of the heart . . . steady and strong . . . suffused by love and gratitude . . . breathing your breath through the heart . . . staying in this place of peace and beauty as long as you wish . . .

(pause)

And knowing you can return here any time . . . just by closing your eyes . . . and placing your hand over your heart . . . and remembering . . .

And so . . . whenever you are ready . . . you can, very gently and with soft eyes . . . allow yourself to come back into the room . . . knowing in a deep place that you are better for this . . .

And so you are . . .

This next exercise is designed to increase your sense of connectedness and ability to resonate with the world of nature.

If you spend a moment looking it over, you will no doubt see how the concepts from David Bohm's implicate order are embedded in this imagery. But I don't recommend your thinking about this while you are actually experiencing the imagery—there's no need to, and even a small amount of analysis can interfere with your experience. Save the cogitating for later, after you've written down the raw data of your impressions immediately after the exercise.

If you choose to listen to this imagery as a recorded narrative, make sure to let *it* guide *you* as you listen. Remember, you want to stay in a relaxed, receptive state of mind, while the imagery does the proactive work for you.

And finally, if you're someone who has trouble making small choices—in this case, the imagery asks you to pick a favorite place in nature—just arbitrarily choose a place before you begin, telling yourself that any place will do, and it doesn't have to be your most favorite place ever.[4] You may find that after you are well under way, the place will switch on you anyway. If it does, let it. It just means that your unconscious is on to something. Follow its lead.

IMAGERY TO RESONATE
WITH SOMETHING IN NATURE
(approximately 10 minutes)

To begin with, see if you can position yourself as comfortably as you can, shifting your weight so that your body is well supported and comfortable . . . and arranging it so that your head, neck, and spine are aligned . . .

And settling fully into your body . . . just dropping your aware-ness down into it . . . as you take a nice, deep, full, cleansing breath . . . inhaling as fully as you comfortably can . . . all the way down into the belly if you can . . . and breathing out as fully as possible . . . gently and easily . . . (pause) . . .

And again, breathing deeply, all the way down into your ab-domen . . . and maybe even feeling it rise, the way it does when you sleep . . . slowly and gently . . . and then releasing the breath with the exhale . . .

And this time, as you breathe in . . . sending the warm energy of the breath to any part of your body that's tense or sore or tight . . . and feeling it warm and loosen and soften all around and through the tension . . . and releasing it with the outbreath . . . (pause) . . . so that more and more, you can feel your breath moving toward all the tight places . . . softening them . . . and breathing them out . . .

And noticing any distracting thoughts that might come into your mind . . . and breathing those out, too . . . so that for just a moment, your mind is empty . . . for just a split second, it is free and clear space . . . and you are graced with stillness . . .

And becoming aware, in a friendly but detached way, of any emotions that might come up to the surface . . . and releasing those, too, with the outbreath . . . so that more and more, you can feel re-laxed and easy, peaceful and still . . . like a lake with no ripples . . .

And now, if you would, imagining a place . . . preferably out-doors . . . where you feel safe and peaceful . . . a place you used to go to . . . or still go to now . . . or somewhere you've always wanted to be . . . by the ocean or in the woods or up in the mountains . . . it doesn't matter . . . just so that it's a place that feels good and safe and peaceful to you . . .

And allowing the place to become more and more real to you . . . in all its dimensions . . . looking around you . . . enjoying the colors . . . the scenery . . . watching the play of light and shadow . . . looking over to your right . . . and over to your left . . . seeing all there is to see . . . all the way to the horizon, if there is one . . .

And feeling whatever you're sitting against or lying upon . . . whether you're leaning against a friendly old tree . . . or maybe you're lying on fragrant, sweet grass that's softly stirring . . . or perhaps you are walking in the woods, and feeling the slippery texture of a pine-needley forest floor beneath your feet . . . or there might be wet sand oozing between your toes, and gentle waves lapping at your ankles . . . or perhaps you're just sitting on a nice, warm rock in the sun . . .

And listening to the sounds of the place . . . birds singing . . . the rustling of the wind through the leaves . . . or maybe it's the steady sound of crickets in the night . . . or the powerful crash of ocean waves . . . perhaps it's the gentle, soothing sound of a bubbling brook . . . just so your ears can become attuned to hearing all the beautiful sounds of your place . . . that is so safe and peaceful to you . . .

And smelling its rich fragrance . . . whether it's the sharp, bracing scent of salt sea air . . . the soft, heavy fullness of flowers . . . the pungent dark green smell of peat moss in the forest . . . sometimes the air is so redolent you can almost taste it on your tongue . . .

And feeling the air on your skin . . . maybe crisp and sharp and dry . . . or soft and balmy and wet . . . just so you're letting your skin enjoy the presence of this place . . . that is so safe and peaceful to you . . . and letting its healing magic soak all the way into your skin . . . penetrating all the way down into your bones . . . all the way down into each and every cell . . .

And feeling your heart fill with gratitude for such stunning beauty . . . soaking into every part of you . . . each slow, pulsing

beat of your heart drumming out its strong, steady gratitude . . .
saluting the beauty all around you . . .

So you're just collecting love and gratitude in your heart, and
sending it out to your special retreat . . . each powerful, rhythmic
beat pulsing out its thanks . . . resonating outward in slow and
gentle waves . . . offering a blessing from the powerful drum of
your heart . . . pulsing love and gratitude out all around you . . .
and seeing it radiate outward . . . reaching into every corner of
this place . . . that is so nourishing to you . . .

(pause)

Giving your thanks, and feeling the place respond with its own
powerful, loving pulse . . . and vibrating it back into you . . . with
its own resonating music . . . answering you that you are welcome
. . . and thanking you again . . . back and forth . . . pulse to pulse,
perfectly synchronized . . . where the giver becomes the receiver
. . . and the receiver becomes the source . . .

(pause)

Dissolving into this pulsing splendor . . . and becoming one
with this beauty . . . one loving, pulsing heart, soft and slow and
rich and full . . . nothing but this . . .

(longer pause)

And so, whenever you are ready . . . very gently and carefully
. . . feeling your heart beating in your chest, slowly and steadily
. . . your feet on the floor or your body in the chair . . . supported,
safe and comfortable . . . relaxed and easy . . . you can very gently
and with soft eyes, allow yourself back into the room . . . knowing
in a deep place that you are better for this . . .

And so you are . . .

For this next imagery exercise, choose a question you might have
about yourself or your life. You can just hold the question in your
mind and acknowledge it to yourself, or you can write it down
on paper before you begin. Most people find writing it down to
be most effective.

Start with an issue that's been going around and around in your mind, something that's been niggling at you for some time but that your analytic mind hasn't been able to solve. Be sure to cast it as a *specific* question at the very beginning, such as "What do I need to do differently in this relationship?" or "What will help me finish this long-overdue project?" or "Where is my life going now?" or "What is my daughter needing from me right now?"

You can use this exercise again and again, but each time, limit yourself to one question, and don't get ahead of yourself during the exercise. The only potential problem from repeatedly using this or any exercise like it is that your rational mind might want to take charge and orchestrate the imagery with its own "logical" solutions, since it now knows what lies ahead in the narrative. But remember, if your analytic mind could have solved this issue for you, it would have done so by now. It's time for the left brain to step aside and give your right brain a crack at the problem.

So just stay with the imagery as it unfolds, moment by moment and step by step. If you can do this, your right brain will rediscover it freshly each time and will conjure up unique and appropriate imagery solutions—plain or encoded—for each situation that you bring to it.

I say "encoded" because it's possible that you'll receive symbolic answers that may or may not make immediate sense to you. The right side of the brain loves metaphors and symbols and can be at its most ingenious when offering them up as solutions. Try to remember them and record them exactly *as is*— you want to avoid the "secondary elaboration" that distorts your answer. Rather than trying to figure out immediately what the symbol means, it's often best to just keep playing with it for a while, suspending analysis until the meaning becomes clear to you spontaneously. And keep in mind, the more surprising and "from out of left field" the images are, the more likely they are to be authentic, psi-derived information.

As with the other exercises, the imagery that follows is designed to open your heart and temporarily dissolve your
boundaries. In this energetic state of boundless fluidity, floating on the vast sea of the nonlocal mind, we can gain access to
wisdom that might be denied us when we are more caught up
in our everyday, concrete, three-dimensional reality.[5]

IMAGERY TO DISSOLVE INTO
UNIVERSAL WISDOM
(approximately 12 minutes)

*To begin with, call to mind the question that you have . . . holding
it lightly as you position yourself as comfortably as you can, shifting your weight so that you're allowing your body to be fully supported . . .*

*And taking a nice deep cleansing breath . . . inhaling as fully as
you comfortably can . . . and sending the warm energy of the
breath to any part of your body that's sore or tense or tight . . . and
releasing the discomfort with the exhale . . . so that you're letting
your breath go to all the uncomfortable places . . . letting it warm
and loosen and soften them . . . and then gathering up the discomfort . . . and breathing it out . . .*

*So that more and more . . . you can be safe and comfortable,
relaxed and easy, watching the cleansing action of the breath . . .
with friendly but detached awareness . . .*

*And any unwelcome thoughts that come to mind, those, too, can
be sent out with the breath . . . released with the exhale . . . so that
for just a moment, the mind is empty . . . for just a split second, it is
free and clear space . . . and you are blessed with stillness . . .*

*And any emotions that are rocking around inside . . . those,
too, can be noted, and acknowledged, and sent out with the breath
. . . so that your emotional self is still and quiet, like a lake with no
ripples . . .*

*And now, if you would, imagining a place where you feel safe
and peaceful and easy . . . a place either real or imaginary . . .*

somewhere you used to go . . . or somewhere you go to now . . . or someplace you've always wanted to be . . . it doesn't matter . . . just so it's a place that feels good and safe and peaceful to you . . . and if many places come to mind, just give yourself permission to choose one of them for now . . . knowing that it doesn't matter which one . . . and what you choose might even change of its own accord later on . . .

And allowing the place to become real to you in all its dimensions . . . looking around you . . . over to your left . . . taking the place in with your eyes . . . enjoying the colors, the scenery . . . and over to your right . . . and seeing what's there . . . so you're just familiarizing yourself with the place . . . that is so safe and peaceful to you . . .

And feeling whatever you are sitting against or walking upon . . . whether it's sand or grass . . . a pine-needley forest floor . . . perhaps you're indoors, in a soft, cozy armchair . . . or maybe you are outside, sitting on a nice, warm rock in the sun . . .

And listening to the sounds of the place . . . birds chirping or waves crashing . . . perhaps it's the soft rustle of the wind moving through the leaves . . . or the music of a bubbling brook . . . just so your ears can become attuned to the wonderful sounds of your place . . .

You might feel a breeze blowing . . . crisp and dry . . . or balmy and wet . . . or the gentle warmth of the sun soaking into your face . . . just so you're letting your skin enjoy the wonderful presence of this place . . . that is so safe and peaceful to you . . .

And smelling its rich fragrance . . . whether it's the soft, full scent of flowers . . . or the invigorating crispness of salt sea air . . . the pungent smell of peat moss in the forest . . . or the heady sweetness of meadow grass . . .

And as you become attuned to the safety and beauty of your place . . . feeling thankful and happy to be there . . . you begin to feel a kind of tingling . . . a pleasant, energizing something in the air all around you . . . something that contains expectancy and excitement . . . a sense that something wonderful is just about to happen . . . *and you might even smile to yourself, because perhaps you haven't had that feeling for a while* . . . *but now you do know with some certainty that there is magic in this place* . . . *and that something wonderful is just about to happen* . . .

And as that certainty settles around you . . . *you notice from somewhere above you a slender ray of light* . . . *shining down and illuminating a small circle, maybe five or six feet in front of you* . . . *a powerfully bright ray of light, humming with its own intensity* . . . *spotlighting a circle of your special place with exquisite brightness* . . . *highlit definition* . . . *vibrating color* . . . *illuminating everything it touches with a fresh, new beauty* . . .

And as your eyes become accustomed to the powerful, vibrant light . . . *you watch, surprised but not surprised, as the circle of light begins to widen* . . . *opening to include more and more of your special retreat* . . . *highlighting and intensifying more and more of its beauty, crisply and clearly* . . .

And you watch with a sense of gentle wonder for such stunning beauty . . . *as the circle enlarges* . . . *and as the air it shines through intensifies, almost singing with its own energy* . . . *everything it reaches coming alive with color* . . . *glowing, dancing, vibrating in its own energy* . . .

And you watch with a peaceful kind of joy as the circle widens further . . . *and approaches you with its generous energy* . . . *feeling it touch you, tingling and dancing on your skin* . . . *softly penetrating your head, neck, and shoulders* . . . *moving down through your body, all around and through muscle and tissue and bone* . . . *down into each and every cell* . . . *energizing you* . . . *filling you* . . .

Feeling the vibrant energy of the light, working its magic deep inside your body . . . *and, hands over your heart, you can sense a shift happening on the inside* . . . *as you feel the light move with deliberate intelligence into the center of your chest* . . . *feeling the warmth collecting all around and through your heart* . . . *cleansing and clearing* . . . *kneading and softening any tightness that might be lodged there* . . . *easing sorrow* . . . *lifting heaviness* . . .

Feeling the vibrant warmth gathering in your heart . . . and overflowing into the surrounding spaces of your body . . . spilling over and filling your chest and torso . . . warming and suffusing your back and belly . . . softly pulsing into every limb . . . up into your shoulders and neck . . . down into your feet and toes . . . until your whole body is resonating with this powerful, loving energy . . .

And feeling your heart responding with its own opening . . . softly expanding, like the velvety petals of a rose, gently unfurling . . . radiating a fragrance of love and gratitude . . . suffusing your whole body . . . a soft warmth pulsing into every corner . . . your whole being alive with radiant energy . . .

And vibrating out into the beauty of your surroundings . . . feeling boundaries dissolve, as you become part of the huge, vibrant song of the place . . . melting into it . . . dissolving into pure, pulsing color . . . into dancing energy . . . glistening light . . . merging into splendor . . . (pause)

Floating in a deep and abiding peace . . . pulsing in the vast quiet and stillness . . .

You may be aware of flashes of information dancing with you . . . the sudden pulsing of a color or an image . . . here and then gone . . . or the quick emergence of a phrase . . . a voice . . . a bar of music . . . or, like the flash of a strobe light, an idea might appear . . . and disappear just as quickly . . . there might be a split-second flash of a feeling . . . a fragrance . . . a face or a presence . . . or there might just be the dancing energy . . . pulsing in the vastness . . .

(long pause)

And whenever you are ready . . . you can begin to gather back into your body . . . getting denser, more solid as you feel yourself pulling back in . . . settling comfortably into the welcoming places of your body . . . gathered in and settling down . . . back home in your body again . . . feeling your feet, your hands, your bottom, your back . . .

Understanding that now or later, something is coming to guide you . . . a flash or pulse of something that may or may not make sense to you . . . but sooner or later, when the time is right, it will . . .

And so, peaceful and easy, you watch as the vibrant, humming light gently begins to contract into itself . . . becoming a smaller and smaller circle . . . until it is gone altogether . . . for now . . .

And you once again find yourself in your special retreat . . . although perhaps the colors around you are brighter . . . the sounds more vivid . . . the air more intense . . . and you may still feel a soft warmth pulsing in the center of your chest . . . and the powerful field of loving, protective energy all around you . . .

You may have a sense that something powerful has happened . . . and will continue to happen, with or without your conscious thinking about it . . .

And knowing you can call forth this place and the vibrant, humming light whenever you wish . . . you can once again feel yourself sitting in your chair or lying down . . . and very gently and with soft eyes, allowing yourself to come back into the room . . . knowing in a deep place that you are better for this . . .

And so you are . . .

This next imagery exercise is also designed to offer fresh solutions to old questions. It's a more elaborate exercise, in that it uses more layers of imagery to set up the request for intuitive information. You can use these two exercises alternately, or you might find that one of them works better for you.

IMAGERY FOR RECEIVING AN ANSWER AS A GIFT[6]

To begin with, please arrange it so that you're comfortable, either sitting or lying down, so that your head, neck, and spine are aligned. See if you can take a moment to shift your weight, so that you're feeling well supported and comfortable . . .

And settling fully down into your body . . . taking a full, deep, cleansing breath . . . (pause) . . . and exhaling as fully as you comfortably can ... (pause) ... and another ... breathing deeply, down into the belly if you can ... filling your abdomen ... and breathing out, fully and completely ...

And once more, breathing in ... and this time, imagining that you are sending the warm energy of your breath to any part of your body that might be tense or tight or sore ... and releasing the tension with the exhale ... so that you can feel your breath going to all the tight, tense places ... loosening and softening them ... and then, gathering it up and breathing it out ... so that more and more, you can feel safe and easy ... relaxed and comfortable ... with the cleansing action of the breath ...

And any unwelcome thoughts that come to mind ... those too can be sent out with the exhale ... so that for just a moment, the mind is empty ... for just a split second, it is free and clear space, and you are blessed with stillness ...

And any emotions that are rocking around inside ... those too can be noted, and acknowledged, and sent out with the breath ... so that your emotional self can be still and quiet, like a lake with no ripples ...

And now ... if you would ... directing your attention inward ... focusing your attention on your heart ... curious about how it feels there ... inside and around your heart ... with all the gentle, curious focus you can bring to bear ... and perhaps even putting the flat palm of your hand over it ... to help you focus your attention even further ...

And just keeping your awareness there ... connecting to the powerful rhythms of your heart ... sensing it pulsing life all through your body ... strong and steady ... as you resonate with the powerful beat of your heart ...

And now beginning to breathe through your heart ... sensing that the breath is actually coming in through your heart ... (pause) ... and breathing out through your heart ... soft and warm and steady ...

So you can begin to feel a kind of warmth and fullness gathering all around your heart ... very soft and rich and full ... as *you continue to focus your attention there . . . and breathe your breath there . . . right through the center of your heart . . . allowing feelings of love and care to collect there . . . letting gratitude fill you . . .*

(pause)

Still breathing through your heart . . . and perhaps beginning to notice the feel of the air immediately around you . . . perceiving a subtle energy, a bristle of aliveness . . . like a gently vibrating cushion of energy . . . softly surrounding and protecting you . . . and perhaps even sensing its sparkling dots of color . . . or hearing a gentle, humming sound . . . tingling energy on your skin . . .

Breathing through the heart, and sending the energy of the outbreath into this living, pulsing cushion of protective energy . . . adding to its density and size . . . making it more and more palpable . . . perhaps even feeling it tingle and vibrate all around you . . . while inside, you can feel safe and protected . . . able to take in what is nourishing to you . . . but protected from whatever you don't want or need . . .

And now . . . imagining that this cushion of energy is drawing to it all the love and sweetness that has ever been felt for you by anyone at any time . . . feeling it pull in all the caring and loving-kindness that has ever been sent your way . . . every prayer and good wish . . . permeating and filling the field of energy around you . . . pulling it all in like a powerful magnet . . . calling every good wish home . . .

And perhaps even sensing the presence of those who have loved or nurtured you . . . just the ones you want with you . . . people from your life . . . alive or long gone . . . or perhaps special animals, guardian angels, magical beings . . . it doesn't matter . . . just so you feel their protection and support . . . those who believed in you . . . who loved and protected you . . . or guided you well

. . . and maybe even feeling them around you now . . . perhaps catching a fleeting glimpse of them . . . or hearing a voice . . . or catching a familiar, well-loved scent . . . a gentle touch on the shoulder . . .

And feeling the soft expansion, all around and through your heart . . . warm and rich and full . . . as you breathe in all the love and caring, all the protection and support . . . and breathe out your love and gratitude . . . and the field of energy around you expands even farther . . .

And perhaps even feeling a slight shift . . . all around and through your head . . . a gentle opening along the plates of the skull . . . as a ring of soft, violet energy dances and vibrates all around your scalp . . . like a magical turban of vibrating lavender light . . . gently massaging and soothing the forehead . . . and all around the scalp . . . just above the ears . . . and all the way around to the back of the skull . . . a pulsing, tingling, violet light . . .

And as you look up, you can see from a distance, someone coming toward you . . . perhaps looking familiar . . . or perhaps not . . . but clearly radiating love and protection and support . . . approaching you, and becoming more and more visible . . . holding something for you that you can't quite see . . . but you know somehow that it's a gift . . . a gift that's specially covered and wrapped . . . something to help you with your puzzle, your question . . . and knowing that this is assistance from the highest place, and for your greatest good . . .

And as it is lovingly placed before you . . . you watch, surprised but not surprised . . . as this loving messenger, looking warmly at you with gentle, smiling eyes, slowly begins to unwrap it for you . . .

(pause)

Something to show you what you need to see . . . to give you a new way of looking . . . a gift for you . . . and what you discover under the wrapping may make sense to you . . . or it may not . . . it might be a complete surprise . . . or very mysterious . . . something very plain and simple . . . or quite familiar . . . it doesn't matter . . . because you can keep it and hold it and examine it again and again . . . from every angle . . . until you see what you need to see . . . and know what you need to know . . .

Able to turn it in your hands . . . and feel its texture . . . catch its scent . . . or hear its sound . . . yours to keep . . . a powerful gift . . . offered freely, and without strings . . . just a gift . . .

And still smiling, the bearer of your gift bows and, with a long and deep look of care and understanding, returns to wherever it came from . . . and you watch the figure recede, feeling peaceful and easy . . . knowing you can call back your visitor whenever you wish . . .

And so . . . still breathing deeply and easily . . . still aware of the warmth in the center of your chest, and still sensing the protection all around you . . . you can once again feel yourself in the center of your body . . . strong and peaceful and steady . . . feeling your body in the chair . . . your feet on the ground . . . your breath in your belly . . .

And very gently, and with soft eyes . . . allowing yourself to come back into the room whenever you wish . . . knowing in a deep place that you are better for this . . .

And so you are . . .

What follows next is a much quicker exercise that you might want to use for questions that require a quick and simple yes-or-no answer. It encourages you to check in with your best friend and your most reliable and trustworthy ally—your body. Once you are tuned into it, you'll find your body a source of constant and profound wisdom. And like any true friend, it won't lie to you.

The key, as always, is to learn to pay attention to subtle cues. Some people are naturally adept at picking up this kind of kinesthetic information through their bodies; others may need a little practice. Recognizing this information is a skill worth having. Not only does it help with picking up psi data, but it can help you stay strong and healthy. You will learn to recognize when you start to go physiologically out of balance—before you have an unpleasant symptom to contend with.

This is an excellent exercise to help you develop the habit of checking inward for guidance during the day. It's quick and reliable, and it works equally well for big and small decisions— anything from "Should I accept this lunch date?" and "Is this a safe street to walk down?" to "Do I want to be doing this for the rest of my life?" and "Is this person good for me?"

The key is this: when your body says yes, you will feel a subtle expansion, a comfortable, gentle release somewhere inside, usually in your chest or abdomen, sometimes in your legs, neck, or shoulders, and sometimes all over. On the other hand, when your body is telling you no, you'll get a subtle tightening, a contraction or a holding back. This may or may not be accompanied by an emotional component that matches the physical feeling of expansion or constriction. Try it. It may take you a while to train yourself to perceive the difference between your body's yes and no, but once you've got it, this skill will stand you in good stead for the rest of your life, keeping you out of trouble and steering you where you need to go.

Have your yes-or-no question ready before beginning this exercise. If possible, write it down.[7]

IMAGERY FOR ASKING THE BODY YES OR NO
(approximately 6 minutes)

To begin with, see if you can position yourself as comfortably as you can, shifting your weight so that you're allowing your body to be fully supported. Try to arrange it so your head, neck, and spine are straight . . .

And taking a deep, full cleansing breath . . . (pause) . . . exhaling as fully as you comfortably can . . . (pause) . . . and again, another deep, full breath . . . all the way down into your belly if you can . . . and again, breathing out . . . (pause) . . .

And now, if you would, gently turning your attention inward . . . focusing inside for just this next while . . . to see how your body is feeling . . . to take a gentle, curious inventory of your insides . . . just a friendly look at what's happening inside your body . . . with the honest, neutral eye of a camera . . .

And feeling where your body might be tight or tense or sore . . . and where it feels loose and soft and open . . . so you're just letting your awareness move around inside your body . . .

Starting perhaps with your head . . . checking to see how it feels inside your head . . . whether it feels tight and busy and congested . . . or comfortable, loose, and open . . . (pause) . . . just noticing what is so . . . no praise, no blame . . . nothing you have to do . . . just noticing . . .

And moving your awareness down into your neck and shoulders . . . curious about any tightness or heaviness there . . . (pause) . . .

And down into your chest . . . continuing to breathe smoothly and deeply . . . sensing how it feels around your heart . . . (pause) . . . aware of any sensation there . . . heavy or tight . . . or spacious and open . . . (pause) . . .

Moving around into the length of the back . . . noticing how your back feels all along the spine . . . (pause) . . . all the way down to your tailbone . . .

And coming back around . . . to see how it feels inside your belly . . . continuing to breathe deeply and easily . . . and feeling what is happening all through your abdomen . . . noticing in a friendly but detached way any tension you might be holding there . . . (pause) . . .

And moving your awareness down into your bottom . . . seeing how it feels all along your whole pelvic floor . . . (pause)

And down into your legs . . . feeling any tightness or rigidity in the legs . . . (pause) . . . all the way down to your feet . . . all the way down to the tips of your toes . . .

So you're just doing this gentle, curious inventory of the insides of your body . . . noting where it might feel denser, tighter, heavier . . . and where it feels looser, lighter, more open . . .

And taking a deep, full breath ... all the way down into any uncomfortable places ... breathing the warm energy of your breath into the heart of the discomfort ... (pause) ... and breathing it out ...

And again ... sending the breath into the core of the tightness ... letting it warm and loosen and soften all around and through it ... (pause) ... and then breathing the discomfort out ... (pause) ...,

So you're just taking this time to reacquaint yourself with this body of yours ... your oldest friend ... your steadiest companion ... and letting your awareness sink down into it ... letting your spirit settle all the way down into your body ...

And in this state of soft, open attention ... alert and present ... taking a moment to ask your question ... either quietly to yourself, in your own mind ... or out loud, if that feels right ... (pause) ... and leaving space for your body to answer ...

(pause)

And noticing whatever subtle or fleeting response you get ... from within your chest or belly ... or perhaps from the legs or buttocks or back ... whatever immediate answer is offered to you ... muscles opening or closing ... a feeling of loosening or tightening ... noticing whatever happens, however subtle or bold ... and whatever doesn't ... with friendly but detached interest ...

(pause)

And just to be sure, if you need to, giving yourself the space to ask the question again ... (pause) ... and attending carefully inside ... curious to hear what your body wants to tell you ... and to feel what it wants you to know ...

(pause)

And in case it is still unclear ... taking a moment to ask the question once again ... either aloud or in your own mind ... and making room in your body for the answer ... perceiving any subtle sensations within ... noticing with friendly curiosity its honest response ...

(pause)

And taking another deep, full breath . . . (pause) . . . and with the exhale, sending thanks to your body for its loyalty and wisdom . . . breathing in your gratitude for this, your oldest and staunchest friend . . . your steadiest companion, who has always told you the truth . . . (pause) . . . and breathing out a sense of balance, peace, and well-being . . .

And whenever you are ready . . . very gently and with soft eyes . . . coming back into the room . . . knowing in a deep place that you are better for this . . .

And so you are . . .

This next exercise is designed to help you find a creative solution to a puzzle or problem you've been working on or trying to solve through the use of symbols and metaphors. The problem could be anything—a work problem or an intellectual question, either abstract or concrete. Maybe you need a key to unlock a door you can't seem to open or something to free your creativity or show you a different way of seeing something.

So to start with, decide on the problem or puzzle for which you need a breakthrough and jot it down. Then choose a symbol for it—some metaphoric way of representing the issue. Don't spend a whole lot of time picking the symbol. It can be how the problem seems to you—slippery like an eel or mushy like mud or hard and impenetrable like a wall of concrete. Or the symbol could represent the problem itself—a nasty, destructive virus represented by a death's head or a decaying organization that takes the form of a dessicated fruit. If you draw a complete blank, pick anything—a stone, a flower, a face—and that will work, too. Once you've decided on your issue and your symbol for it, you're ready to begin.

Keep your writing materials close by, and when the exercise is over, record your impressions faithfully, even if they make no sense to you. Often there is great value in returning to this exercise and using it repeatedly, letting it develop and shift over time—*in its own way,* of course.[8]

IMAGERY TO SOLVE A
PROBLEM METAPHORICALLY

(approximately 12 minutes)

To begin with, see if you can position yourself comfortably . . . shifting your weight so you're allowing your body to be fully supported, with your head, neck, and spine straight . . .

And taking a deep, full, cleansing breath . . . inhaling as fully as you comfortably can . . . and as you do, sending the warm energy of your breath to any part of your body that's sore or tense or tight . . . and releasing the discomfort with the exhale . . . so that you can feel your breath going to all the tight, tense places . . . loosening and softening them . . . and then gathering up all the tension and breathing it out . . . so that more and more, you can feel safe and easy, watching the cleansing action of the breath . . . with friendly but detached awareness . . .

And any distracting thoughts or feelings you might have . . . those, too, can be sent out with the breath . . . released with the exhale . . . so that inside, you can be still and quiet . . . like a lake with no ripples . . .

And now, imagining a place . . . where you feel safe and peaceful and easy . . . a place either real or imaginary . . . someplace you've always wanted to go . . . or go to now . . . or used to go to . . . it doesn't matter . . . just so it's a place that feels good and safe and peaceful to you . . .

And allowing the place to become real to you, in all its dimensions . . . looking around you . . . taking the place in with your eyes . . . enjoying the colors, the scenery . . . looking over to your left . . . and over to your right . . .

And listening to the sound of the place . . . birds singing or leaves rustling . . . the sound of crashing waves or a gurgling stream . . . there might be crickets singing, or the steady thrum of rain on a cozy roof . . . just so your ears can become attuned to the special sounds of your place . . . that is so safe and peaceful to you . . .

*And feeling whatever you are sitting against or lying upon . . .
whether it's sand or grass . . . a pine-needley forest floor . . . or a
nice, warm rock in the sun . . .*

*You might feel a breeze blowing . . . crisp and dry . . . or balmy
and wet . . . there might be the subtlest caress of a fragrant, gentle
breeze . . . or perhaps the bracing sharpness of salt sea air . . . or
the heavy sweetness of meadow grass . . . or the pungent mix of
pine and peat moss in the forest . . .*

*And as you become more and more attuned to the safety and
beauty of your place . . . feeling thankful and happy to be there . . .
you might begin to feel a kind of a tingling . . . a pleasant, energizing something in the air all around you . . . something that contains expectancy and excitement . . . a sense that something
wonderful is just about to happen . . .*

*And looking out in front of you . . . just a few feet ahead, you
can see a kind of shimmering in the air . . . like waves of heat rising from a hot desert floor . . . waves of shimmering energy, just a
few feet in front of you . . . turning into a kind of magical, translucent screen . . . but with a certain solidity to it . . .*

*And as you watch the screen with a kind of peaceful curiosity
. . . you gradually become aware of a form appearing on it . . . becoming more and more defined as you watch . . . and you begin to
recognize that this is the symbol you have chosen . . . to represent
your puzzle, your issue . . . showing up on the screen in all three
dimensions . . . becoming more and more defined and crisp and
clear . . . and you notice that you can watch it with a kind of
peaceful, detached curiosity . . . as it slowly starts to turn . . . allowing you to see it from every angle . . . its form, its color . . .
noticing its size and shape and texture . . . you may even hear certain sounds coming from it . . . it might hum or sing or vibrate . . .
it may even have words to speak . . . or a scent all its own . . . so
you find yourself examining it as it turns . . . carefully, and with
all of your attention . . . friendly, detached, and peaceful . . .*

(long pause)

And now, if you would, see if this image on the screen wants to shift or change in any way . . . if it wants to move in any direction . . . change its shape or color or size . . . modulate its sound . . . tell you something . . . or even if it wants to adjust its texture and feel . . . so you're just waiting to see what it wants to do . . . if it wants to do anything . . . neither pushing nor pulling it . . . but just allowing it to transform itself, in its own way . . . in its own time . . .

And it might not want to change itself at all . . . and that's all right too, if it doesn't . . . but if it does . . . and it might . . . just watching the shift occur . . . in a state of calm but curious detachment . . . observing the transformation with all the attention you can bring to bear . . . in a state of peaceful, detached curiosity . . .

Letting it take however long it needs to . . . understanding that it need not go to completion . . . it need not make any sense to you . . .

(longer pause)

And so . . . when you're ready . . . understanding that you can return to this place . . . and the screen . . . and the symbol whenever you wish . . . letting it take however long it needs to take . . . knowing perfectly well that however long it takes will be just the right amount of time . . .

You can begin to let the image fade . . . until the screen is once again empty . . . and then letting the screen begin to shimmer and fade . . .

And once again, very aware of your beautiful surroundings . . . feeling safe and comfortable . . . relaxed and easy . . . although perhaps the colors are brighter . . . the sounds more vivid . . . the air more alive . . .

And knowing you can return whenever you wish . . . you can breathe deeply into your belly . . . allowing yourself to come back to this reality . . . feeling your feet . . . aware of your whole body . . . and knowing in a deep place that something powerful has

happened . . . that this will be useful to you, sooner or later . . .
that you are better and wiser for this . . .

And so you are . . .

Don't forget to jot down your impressions before moving on.
Otherwise the details are easy to forget. Besides, they may make
sense to you later rather than sooner.

ψ ψ ψ

What follows is an imagery exercise for helping you understand
and connect with another person. It is designed to help you gain
insight, empathy, and compassion toward someone else and, in
so doing, to clarify or shift your attitude toward that person.

This exercise is an especially powerful tool for changing attitudes by providing a direct experience of empathy. It can help
you gain insight and understanding into someone in your
everyday world with whom you're at loggerheads. And it can
also be used to reconnect with someone you miss or with someone who is long gone but whom you wish you'd known better.

But bear in mind that if you're not ready to resolve your
feelings toward this other person or to get to know them better,
you'll probably have trouble completing this exercise. If that
happens, no harm done: in fact, it's useful to know that you
aren't ready to work on improving a relationship. Instead,
choose someone else for the exercise, and come back to the
more challenging relationship when you are truly ready.

So choose someone you would either like to understand
better, empathize with more, or connect with more strongly.
(The person may change in the middle of this exercise, if your
unconscious thinks it has a better idea about who this should
be. If this happens, humor your unconscious—it's pretty smart
about these things and usually *does* have a better idea.) And
please don't spend too long trying to decide who this person
should be; you're best off choosing one of the very first people
that comes into your mind.[9]

IMAGERY TO GAIN INTUITIVE
INSIGHT INTO ANOTHER
(approximately 11 minutes)

To begin with, see if you can position yourself comfortably . . . shifting your weight so you're allowing your body to be fully supported and your head, neck, and spine are straight . . .

And taking a deep, full, cleansing breath . . . inhaling as fully as you comfortably can . . . and as you do, sending the warm energy of your breath to any part of your body that's sore or tense or tight . . . and releasing the discomfort with the exhale . . . so that you can feel your breath going to all the tight, tense places . . . loosening and softening them . . . and then gathering up all the tension and breathing it out . . . so that more and more, you can feel safe and easy, watching the cleansing action of the breath . . . with friendly but detached awareness . . .

And any distracting thoughts or feelings you might have . . . those, too, can be sent out with the breath . . . released with the exhale . . . so that inside, you can be still and quiet . . . like a lake with no ripples . . .

And now, imagining a place . . . where you feel safe and peaceful and easy . . . a place either real or imaginary . . . somewhere you used to go . . . or have always wanted to be . . . or someplace you go to now . . . it doesn't matter . . . just so it's a place that feels good and safe and peaceful to you . . .

And allowing the place to become real to you, in all its dimensions . . . looking around you . . . taking the place in with your eyes . . . enjoying the colors, the scenery . . . looking over to your left . . . and over to your right . . .

And listening to the sounds of the place . . . birds singing or leaves rustling . . . the sound of crashing waves or a gurgling stream . . . there might be crickets singing . . . or the steady thrum of rain on a cozy roof . . . just so your ears can become attuned to the sounds of your place . . . that is so safe and peaceful to you . . .

And feeling whatever you are sitting against or lying upon . . . whether it's sand or grass . . . a pine-needley forest floor . . . or a nice, warm rock in the sun . . .

You might feel a breeze blowing . . . crisp and dry . . . or balmy and wet . . . there might be just the subtlest caress of a fragrant, gentle breeze . . . or perhaps the sharpness of salt sea air . . . or the heavy sweetness of meadow grass . . . or the pungent mix of pine and peat moss in the forest . . .

And as you become more and more attuned to the safety and beauty of the place . . . feeling thankful and happy to be there . . . you might begin to feel a kind of a tingling . . . a pleasant, energizing something in the air all around you . . . something that contains expectancy and excitement . . . a sense that something wonderful is just about to happen . . .

And looking out in front of you . . . just a few feet ahead, you can see a kind of a shimmering in the air . . . the way that heat looks when it's rising from the desert floor . . . waves of energy, maybe five or six feet in front of you . . . turning into a kind of a magical, translucent screen . . . becoming more and more substantial and defined as you look at it . . . a three-dimensional screen . . .

And as you watch the screen with a kind of peaceful curiosity . . . you gradually become aware of a human form beginning to appear on it . . . becoming more and more defined . . . until the image of a person is quite clear to you . . . and you can see that this is the person you've been thinking of . . . the one you'd like to resolve things with . . . or feel more connected to . . . or gain some clarity about . . . someone in your life now . . . or someone long gone . . . or perhaps even someone you never knew . . . but you can watch as this person begins to appear on the screen . . . in whatever characteristic posture they have . . . wearing whatever it is that they wear . . . doing whatever it is that they do . . . becoming more and more clear in every detail . . .

And surprised but not surprised, you see that you can softly and easily enter the screen . . . to have a closer look . . . undetected by them, you can just slip into the screen . . . and have a slow and curious walk around them . . . with a kind of detached, curious interest . . . seeing them from every angle . . . the profile . . . and the back . . . and the other side . . .

And experiencing the feel of the air around them . . . the sounds of the breathing or the voice . . . the smells that surround them . . . so you're just slowly moving around them . . . experiencing a rich, full awareness of them . . . with all of your senses . . .

And now . . . in the safe, magical space of the screen . . . asking permission, for the sake of your own growth and understanding . . . for your peace of mind . . . asking permission to slip past the boundaries of your own skin, and to move your awareness into the body of this other person . . . slipping gently and easily into this other body . . . and breathing with their breath . . . for just a brief while . . .

And if you find yourself holding back and resisting, just gently noting it and allowing yourself to soften all around it . . . for the sake of understanding more . . . to learn what you need to know . . . just an experiment . . . to feel what it is like to be in this other body . . . breathing with this other breath . . . looking down and seeing the hands and the feet . . . the clothing . . .

And feeling what is happening in the heart . . . (pause) . . . all through the belly . . . (pause) . . . in the muscles of the back and the neck . . . (pause) . . . inside the legs . . . (pause) . . . just open and curious as to how it is in here . . .

And seeing out from these eyes . . . what the world looks like from here . . . what it sounds like . . . and feels like . . . as you breathe with their breath . . . and feel with their feelings . . .

(longer pause)

And perhaps even seeing you over there . . . with this pair of eyes . . . what you look like . . . sound like . . . how you seem . . . from this awareness . . . from this body . . . feeling what it feels like to be looking over at you . . . while breathing this breath . . . gently and easily allowing yourself the space to experience this . . . in the safe, magical space of the screen . . . with friendly but detached awareness . . .

(longer pause)

And now . . . softly and easily . . . respectfully wishing this body good-bye . . . with whatever thoughts and wishes you feel are right . . . saying good-bye to this other . . . grateful for the opportunity to have been here . . . to gain some wisdom . . . or compassion . . . as you gently move back into your own body . . . reinhabiting your own skin, fully and easily . . . breathing deeply into your own belly . . . exhaling fully from your own nose and mouth . . . feeling fully the familiar comfort of being back home . . .

And with gratitude for your ability to move so easily back and forth . . . and for the power and reach of your own vast mind and spirit . . . for your ability to gain wisdom and compassion, so simply and easily . . . you can step out of the magical, translucent screen . . . and back into your special, peaceful retreat . . .

Again taking in the beautiful sights and sounds and fragrances . . . the nourishing feel of the place on your skin . . . as you watch the shimmering screen fade . . .

Understanding that you can return whenever you wish, to further the work you have already done . . . with this person or with someone else . . . to open your heart and mind further . . .

And so, feeling comfortable and easy, very gently and with soft eyes, you can return to the room whenever you are ready . . . knowing in a deep place that you are better for this . . .

And so you are . . .

These next two exercises are designed for you to use with another person. They are very powerful heart-opening exercises and will help you get in touch with your own limitless capacity for unconditional love. These are wonderful exercises not just for couples but also for friends, for other family members, for care givers and the people they are looking after, and even for perfect strangers. Using the medium of safe, structured touch potentiates the imagery and takes it even further than usual. The meditative focus of attention is on the other person.

This kind of imagery is usually powerful enough to break through even hard-core resistance and anxiety about surrendering into a receptive, mind-opening state. It will generally engage the involvement of even those who have had trouble using the previous imagery exercises.

These imagery exercises require a rather unusual seating arrangement: sitting choo-choo style, one of you directly behind the other, and both of you facing in the same direction, with the person in the back sitting close up to the person in front. Make sure that each of you is comfortable and well supported.

Don't forget your writing materials. You may have some powerful and noteworthy experiences to jot down.[10]

HEART-TO-HEART PAIRING EXERCISE
(approximately 16 minutes)

Please make yourselves as comfortable as you can . . . sitting with your head, neck, and spine straight . . . and taking a couple of nice, full, cleansing breaths . . . just sending the warm energy of your breath to any part of your body that's sore or tense or tight . . . and letting the breath warm and loosen and soften all the uncomfortable places . . . gathering up the discomfort . . . and letting it out with the exhale . . . so that more and more, you can just watch the healing power of the breath tend to your insides . . . clearing and cleansing . . . soothing and healing . . .

And now, using your mind's eye, imagining a wonderful, protective bubble that shields the two of you from outside distraction, and allows you to be safe and protected inside of it . . . and also imagine, if you would, that the walls of this bubble have a magical ability to draw out of you anything that's left of discomfort or distraction . . . so that anything you might want to discard is auto-

matically absorbed by the walls of the bubble . . . making it even stronger, more protective shielding . . . and inside, you can be still and quiet . . . like a lake with no ripples . . .

And in this magical, safe space . . . I'd like to ask each of you to just let yourselves be . . . breathing deeply and easily . . . and perhaps becoming aware of the energy around your heart . . . aware of the warmth in the center of your chest . . . and letting it softly expand . . . as you breathe, deeply and fully, in and out . . .

And for the person sitting in the back . . . see if you can focus your attention on your partner . . . on the neck or shoulders or back in front of you . . . perhaps focusing on what you might consider to be a particularly vulnerable spot . . . an appealing place that touches your heart . . . and just allowing your own feelings of loving-kindness to collect in your heart . . . for that spot that you're focusing on . . . maybe even sensing something of what the back has carried . . . the burden that the shoulders have known . . . sensing where tension or fear or tightness might be lodged . . . as your heart continues to warm and open and fill with the vast energy of your own loving-kindness . . .

And putting the flat palms of your hands down on the neck or shoulders or back in front of you . . . wherever it seems to feel right . . . and just allowing the warm energy from your heart to move up to your shoulders, down your arms, and into your hands . . . and into your partner . . . to warm and nourish and replenish wherever it is needed . . . letting the energy find the places that need it . . . as you continue to focus on that vulnerable, tender spot . . .

And as for the person sitting in the front . . . see if you can just allow yourself to receive . . . which is, of course, a great gift in and of itself . . . just letting your body soak up the rich, warm energy from the generous heart behind you . . . and letting the energy move through you . . . allowing it to go wherever it is needed . . . and remembering how good it feels to let yourself receive . . . especially when the gift is so freely offered . . .

And the person in back, just feeling the rich, warm energy flowing from the center of your heart, down your arms and into

your hands . . . rich, powerful supplies from the open heart . . .
adding strength and power and fuel for whatever is needed by this
other person . . . no ax to grind . . . no strings or agenda for them
. . . just this energy from the open heart, offered freely and without
reservation . . . and the joy of remembering how good it feels to be
in touch once more with your own generosity . . .

Each of you feeling the richness of the connection . . . open
heart to open heart . . . where the giver becomes the receiver and
the receiver becomes the source . . .

(very long pause—at least 90 seconds)

And whenever you are ready . . . gently allowing yourselves to
disconnect . . . softly and easily . . . and before speaking to each
other, you may each want to jot down some notes on what you
have just experienced . . . any feelings, sensations, images,
thoughts . . . and then take a few minutes to share your experience
with each other. When you are ready, you can complete the exer-
cise by switching roles and repeating this same narrative.

This next exercise builds on the last one and adds a component
that enables you to receive intuitive information for your partner. It is most effectively done with a perfect stranger in a
workshop or study group, for obvious reasons: with a stranger,
you have no previous knowledge to confuse you; it's far less
likely that you'll be misled into logically trying to figure out
what you "should" be saying, based on what you already know;
and you will be more detached about the information you do
receive.

You'll be guided by the narrative to follow the basic guidelines discussed throughout this book. The narrative will help
you clear your mind and focus on the heart-based feelings that
this imagery generates. Through touch and focusing on your
partner, it will be surprisingly easy for most of you to do this.
Then, when the time comes, the narrative will encourage you
to pay attention to any subtle cues, sensations, images, or

thoughts that spontaneously come to you in service to this other person.

Remember, you don't want to interpret the information or try to make sense of it. Just note and report what comes up descriptively. And if you find yourself trying too hard or working too much to logically orchestrate your thoughts, just go back to focusing on your partner and connecting with your loving feelings for that spot on the back of their neck or shoulders. If you reinvolve yourself in doing that, you'll be able to dissipate any performance anxiety or excessive effort that might be getting in your way.

So once again, with your partner, please arrange yourselves choo-choo style, one of you sitting directly behind the other, and both of you facing in the same direction, with the person in back sitting close up to the partner in front. It helps to have a nice, unimpeded view of your partner's back, so if possible choose your chairs and seating positions accordingly.

HEART-TO-HEART PSI ACCESS

(approximately 16 minutes)

Please go ahead and make yourselves as comfortable as you can . . . sitting with your head, neck, and spine straight . . . and taking a couple of nice, full, cleansing breaths . . . just sending the warm energy of your breath to any part of your body that's tense or tight or sore . . . letting the breath soften and warm and loosen any uncomfortable places . . . and breathing the tension out with the exhale . . . so that more and more, you can be relaxed and easy, safe and comfortable, watching the cleansing action of the breath . . .

And now, using your mind's eye, seeing if you can imagine a wonderful, protective bubble that shields the two of you from outside distraction, and allows you to be safe and protected inside of it . . . and also imagining, if you would, that the walls of this bubble have a magical ability to draw out of you anything that's left of discomfort or distraction . . . so that anything you might want to discard is absorbed by the walls of the bubble . . . making it even stronger, more protective shielding . . . and inside, you can be still and quiet, like a lake with no ripples . . .

And in this safe place, I'd like to ask each of you to just let yourselves be . . . continuing to breathe deeply and easily . . . perhaps becoming aware of the energy around the heart . . . aware of the warmth building in the center of the chest . . . and letting it expand, softly and easily, as you breathe . . .

And for the person sitting in the back . . . see if you can focus your attention on your partner . . . on the neck and shoulders and back in front of you . . . perhaps focusing on what you might consider to be a particularly vulnerable spot . . . a place that touches your heart . . . and just allowing your own feelings of loving-kindness to collect in your heart for that place that you're focusing on . . . maybe sensing what the back has carried . . . the burden that the shoulders have known . . . sensing where tension or fear or tightness is lodged . . . as your heart continues to warm and open and fill with the vast energy of your own loving-kindness . . .

And putting the flat palms of your hands down on the neck or shoulders or back in front of you . . . wherever it seems to feel right . . . and just allowing the warm energy from your heart to move up to your shoulders, down your arms, and into your hands . . . and into your partner . . . to warm and nourish and replenish wherever it is needed . . . as you continue to focus on that vulnerable spot . . .

And the person sitting in the front . . . see if you can just allow yourself to receive . . . which is of course a great gift to give in and of itself . . . just letting your body soak up this rich, warm energy from this generous heart behind you . . . and letting the energy move through you . . . allowing it to go wherever it is needed . . . and remembering how good it feels to just let yourself receive . . . especially when the gift is offered so freely . . .

And for the person in back . . . just feeling the warm, rich energy flowing from your heart . . . down your arms . . . and *through your hands ... rich, powerful supplies from the open heart ... just this gift ... offered freely and without strings ... and remembering how good it feels to get back in touch with your own generosity ...*

Enjoying the richness of the connection ... open heart to open heart ... where the giver becomes the receiver and the receiver becomes the source ... pulsing with the beat of one heart ... as you continue to focus on that tender, vulnerable spot ... your heart staying full and warm ... opening yourself to be of service in any way ... to this other being ... to hear or see or feel whatever would be useful ... (pause)

And so you can allow any thoughts or images to come to your awareness ... any sensations, phrases, sights, sounds or symbols ... any colors or music or fragments of ideas ... whatever wants to show up ... however subtle or bold ... and just noting what appears ... in the richness of the connection ... open heart to open heart ... asking only to be of service ... in the vast open spaces of your heart ...

(pause)

And as for your partner ... just allowing and welcoming this assistance ... letting yourself be attended to in this way ... which is a great gift to give ... when you let yourself receive ...

(very long pause)

And so, whenever you are ready to do so ... gently allowing yourselves to disconnect ... to jot down what each of you has seen and heard and felt ... and then sharing these things with your partner ... knowing you can do more if you wish ...

And knowing in a deep place that you are better for this ...

And so you are ...

(Before speaking to each other and sharing your information, you may want to jot down some notes of your raw psi impressions. Remember to keep the data pure, unembellished and unanalyzed. Then switch roles and do the exercise again.)

ψ ψ ψ

So these are the imagery exercises. They replicate the conditions that are experienced just before and during visits from psi and so create an irresistible invitation for psi to come calling. Stay with them and work with them, either on a regular basis—every day or a couple of times a week—or when you need insight or feel ready for some further psi expansion. If you work with them in a study group that meets on a regular basis, that's even better.

And see if you can keep track of the elements that have the most impact on you. After you've grown comfortable with the technique, you may want to create a few imagery exercises of your own, loading up on the parts that work best for you and leaving out the rest.

It's also likely that after a while you won't be needing to do anything this structured, except on especially difficult occasions. The intuitive process will be firmly in place, part of your everyday perceptual experience.

Specific Things You Can Do to Cultivate and Maintain Psi

Now for some specific suggestions about other things you can do to consciously develop your psychic abilities. Follow these tips, and, with or without spectacular, right-brained wiring, you will almost certainly expand your current level of psi functioning.

In the suggestions that follow I've incorporated practices that ensure a more gradual and balanced kind of opening so that the systems that modulate the requisite shifts in energy—the endocrine system and the temporal lobes of the brain, for instance—don't get out of balance as a result. There is no need to tax yourself, either cognitively, psychologically, or physically, while you are developing these capabilities.

I say this because some of the people in my study who underwent periods of rapid, ungrounded expansion suffered at different times from varying amounts of endocrine system anomalies (usually temporary), particularly in the thyroid and adrenal glands. Others had periods of migraine headaches, dizziness, disorientation, and nausea. Often this happened at times of spontaneous, semiconscious psi opening, after trauma, or when the person was pushing too hard, just hell-bent on finding interesting phenomena.

There is no need for debilitating physical effects from this process—quite the contrary. When psi development is pursued carefully and respectfully, with reasonable attention to your physical and emotional needs, it can be an energizing, health-promoting, and self-renewing process.

This is even more true when it is pursued through the doorway of the open heart, where body and spirit meet and coexist. Working in this way enhances your sense of purpose, joy, and connection to all life. But we mustn't forget that the body is the vehicle housing all those shifting vibrations and oscillations, and its requirements must be understood and respected while pursuing this adventure.

So here is my list of things you can do.

1. FOCUS INTENT AND PAY ATTENTION

Simple as it sounds, focusing your conscious intention to develop this skill is a powerful way to activate it. Stating your wish aloud or in your own mind and then just paying attention to the intuitive processes within and around you will expand your psi functioning. Being clear about your desire to do this will automatically organize your thinking and attention and will bring a lot of your energy into coherence. As author and intuition trainer Victor R. Beasley, Ph.D., explains, "Energy follows thought, and that which we focus on expands. . . . We're all hardwired for this ability anyway, so we open to it rather easily with a little attention paid to it."

Similarly, David Davis, Ph.D., a Reston, Virginia, intuition trainer and corporate consultant, recalls, "I always had a sensitivity to it [energy and intuition], but it became much more acute once I made a conscious decision to develop it."

Several of the people I interviewed asked me (somewhat disingenuously, I suspect, since most of them seemed to know the answer already) whether my working on this book had further opened up my intuitive channels. My answer, of course, was yes, very much so: indeed, in the year since embarking on this project, I have become extremely sensitized to my environment and the information around me. The amount of psychic information that comes to me now has greatly increased over a year ago. Many factors are involved in this, but one critical one is the simple act of focusing a lot of thought, intention, and attention on the topic of psi.

2. KEEP A JOURNAL

Just as recording dreams helps capture more and more of them for recall, keeping a log of intuitive experiences and recording daily "hits" and "misses" enhances psi. It is a concrete way of focusing your attention and of making what is unconscious, conscious. Without putting them in writing, you might experience several accurate hits in a day but never notice them.

When keeping a journal, you can't help but be impressed at the end of the day when you see the clear evidence of a dozen or so hits; and even more encouraging is the progression in the frequency of hits by the end of a week. This feedback validates the process and motivates you to continue.

You'll also be able to see your patterns: whether or not your psi functioning seems enhanced at certain times of the day, month, or even year; and whether or how it's connected to what you ate, certain emotions you've been feeling, who you've been spending time with, or even your geographic location.

Several of the people I interviewed reported that they used this device to good effect early on in their psychic development and then dropped it once their psi skills were more fully engaged.

3. KEEP LIKE COMPANY

One of the most powerful psi developers seems to be simply spending time, structured or unstructured, with similarly interested friends and colleagues. Because so much of our culture is geared away from giving the right side of the brain its due, it is important—for many of us even necessary—to get validation from a group of people whose view of reality matches our own. As a result, many people seem to gravitate toward others who are on a similar path of psi exploration.

It can be very helpful to join a structured self-help group for a while, and many people form their own meditation, personal growth, and intuition development groups. These generally meet once a week or once or twice a month, and they usually are started by the person who is hungry enough for the companionship of like-minded seekers to take the time and trouble to make the calls and provide the meeting space. Some of these groups use a structured method or curriculum,[1] while others develop their own agenda as they go along.

I remember belonging to one such group years ago, in my neighborhood. We were as diverse a bunch as we could be, we certainly didn't know a whole lot, and we tended to get fascinated with a certain amount of occult hooey that now I wouldn't touch with a ten-foot pole. (We jokingly referred to ourselves as The Spook Group, because a couple of the conveners were especially interested in connecting with ghost phenomena.) Our eccentricities notwithstanding, it was a wonderful, powerful support system that kept each of us from feeling too isolated on our individual quests. And, although we met for only a year or two, our ties are still strong, and some of my closest friends today are from that group. It was an important mutual support system, and we helped one another a lot.

4. FIND GOOD TEACHERS

Another, even more structured way of finding support is to study with a teacher. Many of the people I interviewed learned from mentors, spiritual teachers, and guides. Some had a hard time finding an appropriate teacher, but when they finally did, it felt to them like they were coming home at last.

The structure that a system of teachings and principles offers can provide the grounding that keeps psychic growth in good balance. The best systems tend to be the ones that have been around the longest. Chi kung and tai chi master Ken Cohen, for instance, studied for years with a chi kung master from China as well as with several Native American teachers (most notably Keetoowah Christie and Rolling Thunder of the Cherokee Nation) and with many others. His excellent training is reflected in his powerful, inspired work as a teacher and healer and also in the grounded strength, clarity, and authenticity with which he approaches his work.

A good teacher will provide you with informed feedback and a steady hand to push the learning along but also will slow you down when you are on overload and help you keep your ego in check. Perhaps most important, in the wide-ranging explorations of boundless psi territory, a teacher can provide an ethical system as a grounding structure from which to function. And, of course, the friendships that develop in the learning environment created by a good teacher are powerful and lasting.

You can find the right teacher by keeping your ears open, attending conferences and workshops, listening to presenters, talking to friends, and reading people's books. Make sure to get references from other students you respect, and, above all, trust your own instincts about who would be appropriate for you at this time in your life.

There are some obvious cautions: keep away from the gurus who foster dependency with a teaching style that leads you away from your own sense of power and inner knowing or who behave in ways that violate your personal code of ethics; if you see that they violate even their own stated code of ethics, it is a surefire reason to keep away. Avoid teachers who keep you away from connecting with your fellow students; who teach through humiliation, shame, or fear; who are overly interested in your checkbook; or who discourage you from learning elsewhere. And, of course, even though learning is a lifelong process, don't remain someone's student any longer than necessary. The world is full of teachers to learn from, and you are one of them yourself.

5. SEEK OUT SOLITUDE

A certain amount of time deliberately spent in reflective solitude is essential for psi development for many reasons. First of all, solitude will afford you the stillness and quiet that you need in order to hear your own delicate inner voice. It's hard to direct your attention inward if you are surrounded by external stimulation and are sensitive to it to boot.

Second, you need time to reflect upon your own thoughts and feelings, your own sense of yourself, your motivations and distortions. This keeps you clear and helps keep the information that you are getting free from your own projections. In order to have time to reflect, you need regular time with yourself.

Not surprisingly, there was an extraordinary proportion of only children in my sample of intuitives. When I asked them if they felt that this was a factor in their psi adeptness, they answered yes and connected it primarily to the alone time that being an only child afforded them.

Another good reason to seek out solitude is to recover from overstimulation in the environment. Many people, especially in the beginning stages of increasing their psi sensitivity, can become extremely reactive to the environment and may find themselves far too much at the mercy of other people's moods and needs, of the atmosphere of a room, of the thoughts of the person passing by them, and even of the headache of a lunch partner. Solitude helps one recover balance after this kind of unwelcome overstimulation and is very important to staying grounded.

6. SPEND TIME IN NATURE

One of the best places to seek out solitude is in the natural world, where you can receive both inspiration and grounding at the same time. Most of the people I interviewed had an absolute, rock-bottom need either to visit frequently or else live next to water, woods, or mountains. More people craved the ocean than anything else, but many people also spoke of their need to be close to moving freshwater, the earth, digging in the dirt, lying on the ground, or touching and talking to trees and animals.

Some were quite specific in their requirements: Sue Greer said she needed to live where she could see hawks in the morning; Ken Cohen required being 9,000 feet above sea level on a Colorado mountain; and Mary Sherman needed ocean water; Lake Erie, huge and close by, wouldn't do because it lacked the salt and tidal activity she needed.

People spoke of these settings not as luxuries but as necessities. They experienced nature as a requirement for maintaining balance and attunement and for deriving emotional nourishment. Kathlyn Rhea described feeling a loss of peacefulness when she was away from open space and forest, water and trees. She told me, "Nature is always in balance. . . . The more sensitive you are to picking up the energy around you, the more it makes sense to live in more peaceful surroundings."

Not surprisingly, many people felt that as children they had initially developed their psi abilities by spending a lot of time alone in nature. Even people like Iris Saltzman, who grew up in New York City, gravitated toward spending extended periods of time in city parks; others enjoyed the roofs of their apartment buildings.

7. BE PRESENT AND AWARE

Your skills at tuning in to psi will grow just from greater moment-to-moment awareness of *whatever it is you are doing*. Bringing a single-pointed focus and a quality of being fully present to whatever it is you are doing—whether it's tying your shoes, chopping vegetables, listening to a friend, getting irritated in traffic, or just breathing the air—will help you open your third eye further. After all, psychic ability is really nothing but a kind of *extended awareness, a certain heightened quality of presence and concentration.*

Corporate trainer David Davis describes his way of being "intensely present but unbound" as being very helpful to his ability to perceive psychically. Osteopath Vivian Bochenek talks about the importance of doing just one thing at a time, very consciously and deliberately, when she is resting: drinking tea and *only* drinking tea; gardening and *only* gardening. During these times, she is not thinking about her patients or her list of things to do; she is just bringing all the focus she can to each moment of her tea drinking and her gardening and on all the perceptions and sensations involved. This is her way of meditating.

Similarly, Ken Cohen describes the importance of the quality of awareness in his feeling that "the ordinary and the everyday is filled with mystery and beauty, if we only pay attention." Parapsychologist Rhea White used to have a practice of "walking intuitively" in the woods, where she became so utterly attuned to the rhythms of the trees and the undergrowth she was walking through that she had the timeless feeling that the motion of her body was just blending into the woods, each movement flowing rhythmically into the next.

Interestingly enough, artist Cynthia Gale coined the term *time-stretching* for what happens inside of her when her attention is fixed on creating her ceremonial objects. Her attention becomes so focused on what she is doing that she perceives clock time as stretching out, and she accomplishes great amounts of work in "no time."

Perhaps this sounds familiar. Cynthia's description recalls Itzhak Bentov's discussion of how subjective time expands when our brain wave frequencies slow down under certain meditative conditions. And, of course, this heightened awareness is in fact a form of meditation, an unstructured variety that can be spontaneously applied to whatever it is you are doing.

8. PRACTICE STRUCTURED MEDITATION

For many people, structured meditation is the key to their psychic development. In my survey, meditation was the factor most frequently cited for increasing skill. This is because meditation simultaneously clears and stills the mind, focuses awareness, and, in the case of mindfulness and other popular forms of meditation, turns the attention inward. At the same time it increases discipline, courage, energy, and presence in the meditator.

Even in a busy schedule, sitting quietly once or twice a day for about fifteen minutes is doable and ultimately affords you more time because it focuses your energies. You can practice mindfulness—watching your thoughts, feelings, perceptions, and body sensations as they come up into your awareness and float on out. Or you can focus your attention on a word or a mantra, repeating "Peace" or "I breathe in beauty; I breathe out love." You might prefer just to track your breathing without words or to hold a special image in your mind's eye.

Chicago psychic and teacher Sonia Choquette encourages her students to use a very simple, fifteen-minute technique every day. It's not especially demanding. She has them start by sitting comfortably, with eyes closed, concentrating their awareness on the breath while pleasant music plays in the background. First they inhale to the count of four; then they hold their breath to the count of four; and then they exhale to the count of four. When a comfortable, slow pace is established, she has them concentrate on one simple idea and repeat it again and again—something like "I am at peace" or "I am still and calm."[2]

My favorite kind of meditation for intuitive development, as you've probably noticed by now, is what is sometimes referred to as *mehta* or *loving-kindness meditation.* It entails focusing attention on the heart, focusing the breathing there, and evoking feelings of love and gratitude, usually with the aid of some love-generating imagery or some special memories.

Don't forget that meditation need not be done sitting or lying down. One of the most powerful meditations that I like to use is a walking meditation, where the attention is focused on taking in the sights, sounds, smells, and feel of the environment during a walk, along with the feel of the feet touching and leaving the ground and the breath moving through the body. This kind of meditation works even for people who swear they hate meditating because they get fidgety and agitated trying to harness their minds while sitting still.[3]

And finally, some of the most powerful meditations involve focusing the attention on the practice of certain body movements, coordinated with the breath and frequently with some imagery as well. Yoga, tai chi, chi kung, aikido, karate, and Emilie Conrad-Da'oud's Continuum movements are excellent examples of this kind of meditation.[4] You needn't be an athlete to perform most of them, and the continuum movements are so subtle that they are barely noticeable from the outside.

These kinds of practices serve both to help the mind open to psi and to keep the body and psyche in balance while this takes place, so there is great benefit to this more physical approach. I was impressed with one observation during the course of my interviews: *Invariably, the people in my sample who practiced these more physical meditations on a regular basis had far fewer physical complaints.* As a result, I encourage a daily combination of sitting meditation and physical practice meditation, even if it's only ten minutes of each. And, naturally, more is better.

9. GET PHYSICAL EXERCISE

It is also important as you proceed in your development to keep up (or develop in the first place) your physical strength: to exercise, build muscle mass, and take good care of your physical body. Even simple, regular walking and a little low-demand weightlifting can be extremely helpful.

Rosalyn Bruyere sees channeling energy as an *athletic skill,* one that requires a high-tech body to manage it. For her, this meant losing one hundred pounds, taking up karate, and working with weights. "Mediums traditionally were three-hundred-pound women with hyperinsulinism. It doesn't have to be that way," she says.

Care for the body is needed to balance the growth in psyche and spirit. Not surprisingly, the natural athletes and very physical people in my survey—quite a few dancers and athletes appear in my sample of intuitive people—had the fewest complaints about their bodies, emotions, or hormones going out of balance.

And indeed, imbalances may show up especially in the hormone-producing endocrine system. Miami medical intuitive

Iris Saltzman first called this to my attention, and Sue Greer, Vivian Bochenek, and Rosalyn Bruyere all confirmed that the endocrine system is indeed extra vulnerable, because it is the physical system that mediates between the physical body and the more subtle (etheric) energies around it. As psi capacity opens, more energy comes through the body.

Kathlyn Rhea feels that the adrenal glands are one of the first places in the physical body that respond to emotions and that as we develop psi abilities, we become more and more sensitized to emotions, our own and other people's.[5]

For all these reasons and no doubt others as well, the vulnerable endocrine system needs something to hold it steady during periods of rapidly expanding psi activity, and substantial, regular physical exercise seems to do the job.

Of course, this is not exactly radical news, and it is consistent with what psychiatry tells us about how to go about balancing mood. Most psychotherapists now know to recommend exercise as one of the first lines of defense against mood imbalance, because for many people it can automatically generate, balance, and metabolize hormone levels at a nice, even pace, with only pleasant side effects. However, I want to emphasize the importance of exercise here, because most people don't think of it as having any relevance to opening up psi capability.

10. DEMONSTRATE AWARENESS AND DISCRIMINATION IN EATING AND DRINKING

Occasional fasting or a general policy of not overeating was a device mentioned by several people as one way they supported their psi development; and, conversely, deliberate eating (or eating heavier foods, such as meat) was used as a device to get grounded back into earth time.

Several people developed their own unique diets, born of experimentation and paying close attention to their bodies' physical and emotional reactions to different foods. Usually, this kind of conscious awareness about eating—not obsessive, just attentive—is self-corrective and will balance out nutritional needs and metabolism naturally. Quite a few people found sugars and alcohol extremely toxic, with their sensitivity to these substances increasing with their psi development. Others completely lost their taste for meat. Kathlyn Rhea outlines the vitamins in foods needed for healthy adrenals in her book *Mind Sense.*[6]

Rosalyn Bruyere cautions that in the old Spiritualist ways and culture, too many psychic healers and readers were habituated to using some form of sugar—sweets or alcohol—to ground themselves, but often their metabolism digested the sugar first and never got to the rest of the nutrients, thus producing her legendary three-hundred-pound medium.

Bruyere feels that the intense healing work that she does, running a great deal of current through her body, causes her to quickly exhaust her hormone supplies of serotonin and melatonin, as well as certain minerals. As a result, she supplements her diet with special broths, dark green vegetables, and a lot of minerals and protein. She has learned over the years that carbohydrates are not good for her. This kind of careful attention to the particular dietary needs of her body while she does her healing work has kept her strong, healthy, and charged.

11. KNOW YOURSELF

In order for you to be a trustworthy helper of others and a reliable conveyer of psychic information, it is essential that you be well versed in your own motivations, wishes, and desires and well schooled in your own unique tendencies toward distortion and projection. This is an ongoing process that none of us is ever done with—truly a lifelong project.

Very simply, with receiving and reporting psi information, you must always sort out what is about you and what is about someone else, *in a grounded, reality-based way.* It is not enough to create a self-enclosed intuitive system that presumably sorts things out without any feedback from outside your loop (as in, "My intuition"—or "my inner guidance," "my higher self," or "my spirit guides"—"told me this was your problem, not mine"). So a certain openness to feedback and a respectfulness toward the dissonant perceptions of others are essential to grounded, responsible practice. The best way to avoid arrogantly imposing your internal biases on others is to know what they are.

Many psychics use psychotherapy, mindfulness meditation, or regular introspection with a good, honest friend, support group, or teacher to help with this process. Counselors, therapists, and many care givers are taught structured introspection as part of their professional training, and some people just come by it naturally with a lot of strong, inborn emotional intelligence. But regardless of whatever natural advantages and skills we might have in self-awareness, we can always put more effort into expanding our understanding of the places we are vulnerable to self-deception.

By cultivating self-awareness, you will develop greater clarity and authenticity in your way of being in the world. By eliminating blocks, self-deception, and distraction, you acquire a greater ability to hold and focus your energy. In other words, you have more charisma and personal power.

And, of course, the more charisma and personal power you have, the more it behooves you to cultivate your authenticity and ethical behavior. If you continue faithfully with the process of honest self-discovery and self-assessment, you are much less likely to abuse these powerful side benefits.

12. CHECK IN WITH YOUR BODY

If you keep track of how your body feels when you have an accurate intuitive hit or psychic pop, your skillfulness will naturally increase. There is a built-in biofeedback loop here that goes to work for you. For many people, this involves feeling certain kinesthetic sensations that are unique to them—subtle but discernible bristlings and flowings of energy, like a very mild electrical current. Others will experience more of an emotional feeling of being "on," and still others will have a cognitive sense of unusual clarity of mind. Some experience all three. But almost everybody, especially in the beginning stages when the appearance of psi is more noticeable and dramatic, will be able to identify a signature response or set of responses to the experience of receiving accurate material.

In the same way, there is an identifiable feeling for being "off" that is usually in marked contrast to being "on"—a sense of duller, less focused energy or a feeling of vagueness, confusion, trying too hard, thinking too much, or simply being disconnected from yourself. By tracking and noting both kinds of experiences, the frequency and accuracy of the "on" times will grow, and you'll have a fairly reliable idea of what information you can more likely count on.

13. RELY ON EXTERNAL FEEDBACK TO CHECK YOUR DATA

It is also important to use feedback from external sources to check and supplement your data. This increases your confidence, teaches you about how and when you typically distort, and keeps you from counting exclusively on supposedly unimpeachable spiritual sources.

No one is right all the time. In fact, according to Joe McMoneagle, in most remote viewing experiments, getting hits 65 percent of the time is considered an excellent score. Joe, a remote viewer in the United States government's psychic experiments for seventeen years, illustrated this point when he described the time in 1982 that he successfully located Brigadier General Dozier, who at the time was being held hostage in Italy by the Red Brigade. Although he correctly identified the city (Padua), and the looks of the building (a second-story apartment, over a grocery store), and even the floor plan of the apartment itself, the information still needed supplementing and corroboration from other operatives. "What makes remote viewing information valuable," he says, "is when it's used in conjunction with other sources of information. It's most effective when it's used to key in other collection systems."

Many of the people I interviewed told me that they learned a great deal from being told when they were right and when they were wrong. Healers and medical intuitives like Ken Koles, Mona Lisa Schulz, and Kathlyn Rhea always encourage reliance on traditional kinds of medical consultation to corroborate and amplify their information.

14. SLOW DOWN YOUR PACE

Ceremonial artist Cynthia Gale says, "People can't be psychic when they're hurrying." Indeed, there is something in the nature of unhurried time that lends itself to psi. When we can deliberately adjust our pace so that we can experience time as *abundant* and *now,* we create more space for intuition.

Interestingly enough, an odd phenomenon happens when we do this: we actually wind up having more time in which to get things done. Time stretches out for us, because we have moved into that state of extended *subjective time,* those still points of the pendulum swing in our ever-oscillating bodies that I described in chapter 5.

Cynthia goes on to say, "It's fun dissolving the nonsense we've been taught that time is. I see time as limitless. When I'm in a perspective of timelessness, there's plenty of time, an abundance of it." She is not speaking metaphorically here. All of us who are Cynthia's friends are forever slack-jawed at the amount of art she can produce in a very brief amount of clock time. It seems to just show up overnight, like Rumpelstiltskin's gold.

Laura Chapman, too, describes this phenomenon, in regard to both her healing work and her dancing background: "There is an extended moment where time stretches out, where there is no beginning and no end." This is the consciousness that is so conducive to creativity, to peak performance, and, of course, to psi.

15. PARTAKE IN THE ARTS

Perhaps it is because of these special psi-conducive qualities of extended time, so present in the production and performance of art, dancing, acting, playing a musical instrument, singing, or writing poetry, that so many people involved in these or other creative endeavors are so open to their psychic ability. Of the people I interviewed, only two had no serious involvement whatsoever in any kind of artistic or creative endeavors. And many people were very active in several different, unrelated, artistic fields.

Although everyone was not currently engaged in these creative pursuits, they generally had been for extended periods of time at certain points in their lives. Some felt that, because their creative endeavors, like psi, involved right-brain activity, the creativity had helped them develop psychically. Others felt creativity simply was part and parcel of their intuitive way of operating in the world, and they saw no clear distinction between intuition and creativity. Bryan Christopher, a musical prodigy as a child and a professional dancer as a young adult, believes, "It's all the same. It's all artistic. It's all creative energy. When artists are tortured, it's because they're channeling all this energy that they don't really understand or know how to accommodate. But creating art is basically the same energy as intuition and healing."

Indeed, most of the people in the study saw their creative pursuits as a way of staying in balance, clear, focused, and quiet, and most engaged in at least one form of artistic expression whenever time would allow.

16. BE PLAYFUL AND PLAY GAMES

Testing your psi ability on things that don't matter to you a whole lot is an excellent way of expanding it. So divining which bank teller line is going to open next, who is calling on the phone, whether a letter contains good, bad, or neutral news, or where a parking space is going to show up gives you a chance to test yourself *playfully* and *without attachment* to outcome.

At the same time, games like these provide immediate feedback; within moments you know if you were right or wrong, and this will quickly educate you as to the difference in feeling between each of these two outcomes. Scores of opportunities are available for this kind of play in the course of a day, so it also offers you a very handy and regular form of psychic exercise.

People in my study honed their skills on everything from predicting the commodities market (without actually *investing* in it, of course) to coming up with medical diagnoses on the way to the emergency room. But in every case, the key was that they never became invested in the outcomes they were guessing but instead saw the process as strictly practice—a means of developing their skill and getting a little psychic exercise. It was a game, held lightly and playfully. For this reason, games like these are an excellent training ground for cultivating the attitude of detachment needed for accurate perception when the stakes are higher.

Besides, psi likes to have a good time, and experiences with it often *are* fun. Many intuitives are given to smiling, laughing, and joking during their readings or counseling sessions, as if a running commentary of very amusing observations were coming through from a knee-slapping gang of guffawing spirit guides.

The Reverend Gregory Kehn is often found chortling during a reading. He will usually attribute this to the ironic observations made by one of his clients' guides or his guides. With Greg, the sound advice and helpful wisdom he offers is always laced with humor. Similarly, Cynthia Gale is often smiling and chuckling while she tunes in to psychic information for her friends and clients. She speaks very directly of the importance of maintaining this playful attitude in her work and of how muddy it can become without it. Sometimes, she says, she shuts down altogether, if her lightheartedness, either through fear or stress, is temporarily absent.

Bryan Christopher always looks as though he is having a wonderful time during a reading—his eyes sparkle, his face looks happy and playful, and his descriptions are often framed in gently funny metaphors. Sometimes he will even rub his hands together in anticipatory glee when he begins to speak.

Also, humor and playfulness serve as a kind of automatic corrective device, a way of getting back on track and returning to balance whenever fear, worry, stress, a need to impress, the intrusion of proactive striving, too much investment in outcome, or just plain excess of ego threaten to kill off or distort the flow of psychic information.

17. PRAY

Praying for guidance, clarity, and integrity is an essential part of the process of gaining access to psi. When we seek assistance from a higher source, regardless of how our notion of divinity is packaged, we direct our intention toward staying with what is good, right, and beneficial to the greater whole and the bigger picture. In doing so, we align ourselves with universal energies; we can ride the wave of the infinite, pulsing information field that surrounds and penetrates us. It is always a matter of transcending ourselves in order to gain and accommodate transcendent information; so for many people, prayer does the job.

Without prayer, many of us would be continually bumping up against our egos and contending with so many personal obstacles and agendas to sort through that it would be constant work just to stay clear—perhaps not even worth the trouble. But prayer reminds us that we are not doing this alone—more to the point, that it's not even *about* us.

Just about everyone in my sample prayed, even the more hard-nosed rationalists who were a little embarrassed by spiritual or religious language. But when pressed, they acknowledged that they aligned themselves or prayed to *something* to help them do what was right, in the best way possible. And when I asked the people in my sample the question, "Where do you think this information comes from?" they would answer with some sort of description of God.

18. BUILD SACRED SPACE
AND CREATE RITUAL

It helps to deliberately construct some sort of ritual that defines sacred space as you engage in this process of opening to psi. It can be an actual space—a special area in your home or office that holds some meaningful, ceremonial objects, such as a candle, a statue, a rock, or a feather that has some special encoded meaning for you—or it can mean a specific prayer, meditation, statement of intention, or specially constructed sequence of behaviors that opens and closes your time for seeking out psi. Many counselors and healers use all of these things for the times that they engage in spiritual counseling, intuitive readings, or healing in a structured way.

The rituals or ceremonial space needn't be overt. In fact, you want to avoid doing or saying anything that has too theatrical a quality to it, because if you engage in too much dramatic ceremony, especially in front of other people, you run the risk of getting caught up in *how you look from the outside* and compromising your integrity—a sure kiss of death to intuitive endeavors. Most people engage in ritual activities when they are alone, preparing for their psi-opening work.

Preparing ritually sets your intention in a very concrete way, and it conditions your mind and body to quickly assume the attitude and focus of attention necessary to open up to psychic information. Eventually, with enough use, the sacred space takes on a life of its own and does some of the work for you.

Johanna Caroll describes a special feeling in the room that she has set aside for her telephone work with clients (she likes to use the term *spiritual mentoring* for her practice). "It's very quiet in there but very energized," she says, "with a very intensified feeling of peace, a very strong spiritual presence. It's in the rest of the house, too, but not as strong. When I leave the room it's like I'm stepping down to another level, even though I know there are no stairs, and I'm not doing it physically."

19. TELL THE TRUTH

It's important to make a practice of telling the truth whenever possible. When you cannot do that, try to keep quiet. And if there are times when you feel you simply must lie, then do so *consciously* and with full awareness that you are doing so. If you feel the need to lie, chances are you are ashamed or afraid. The antidote for that is simple: just give yourself permission to notice how you feel with compassion and without judgment.

Psychic awareness is about integrity—about being true to ourselves and our own inner experience. When there is a perfect match among what we think, feel, say, and do, we are in alignment with ourselves and at our most energized and psychically skillful. I suppose it's the psychological equivalent of physically matching the frequencies of our hearts and brains and achieving a standing wave of coherence.

If you stay aware of your process, watching (always, of course, with *kindness and humor*) all the times you struggle with telling the truth on any given day, some interesting things will start to happen. You'll become more truthful, both with yourself and with others, and your level of discomfort from telling mindless, automatic lies will grow. You'll feel stronger, more in tune with yourself, and far less at the mercy of the opinions and choices of others. This will not make you insensitive or selfish, just clearer and stronger. And your psychic ability will become more reliable.

20. OBSERVE THE FABULOUS MACHINATIONS OF YOUR EGO

One of the most important practices you can engage in is watching the amazing workings of your ego, and what great sport that can be! With the same attitude of friendly but detached awareness and humorous attention that you gave to tracking your truth telling, watch all the times you find yourself needing to be noticed, acknowledged, special, needed, powerful, or smart. Track all the times you found it necessary to take credit, disown blame, or raise your stock in someone else's eyes. Gently notice when you do things for effect and the times you feel slighted, overlooked, competitive, or threatened. It is usually these things that constrict our energy and lead to our more mean-spirited behavior, and it's very good just to notice them with clear eyes. Kidding ourselves about our motives only diverts and dilutes our energy, and, when all is said and done, it weakens our efforts.

And, of course, don't forget to notice the times that you let go of all of that ego-driven behavior and act from a place of genuine empathy, generosity, and compassion or from just the sheer joy of expressing yourself.

This exercise in awareness, when done with compassion and humor, keeps the ego nicely in check and, as with truth telling, leads to greater energy, coherence, power, and wholeness.

It is, of course, especially important to cultivate ego watching when your psi skills are growing. Greater access to information gives us more power, and more power *always* requires greater accountability and responsibility.

21. PRACTICE KINDNESS

The regular practice of conscious acts of kindness seems to correspond directly with the development of psi skills. Perhaps that's because of the increased awareness of our oneness with everything in the universe. Maybe they go together because both are connected to slowing down, becoming more present, and savoring the experience of daily living—we all become kinder when we do this.

Certainly kindness accompanies the compassion of living with an open heart. Kindness is concretized empathy. When our boundaries open to include others and we allow ourselves to feel what they feel and see what they see, the natural end result is kinder, more caring behavior.

Bryan Christopher talks about the importance of watching what he thinks so that he is not setting himself apart from others. He says, "I have to constantly remind myself that my humanness is going to want me to separate myself from others. So I watch what I think, not to organize my thoughts in such a way that sets me apart from another person."

Although few of the people I interviewed talked directly about kindness per se, I found their demonstrations of natural kindness and generosity to be extraordinary and very touching. It was reflected in their ample gifts of time, work, ideas, and materials, which they offered freely to help with this book. It also showed up in the generous way they spoke about other people and in their humility about themselves.

And, in keeping with the spirit of these new people and voices in my life, my own day-to-day kindness level seemed to go up a notch or two, particularly with regard to the small things—like *enjoying* letting someone ahead of me in traffic or being patient with an unfocused talker who was having trouble getting to the point. (It has always been easy for me to be kind to people when they were in big trouble, but in the small, daily trials, I'm frequently a curmudgeon, so it was here that the personal changes really showed up.) Increased kindness is also linked to having a sense of expanded time. When we're not hurrying, we're kinder.

Exercising kindness and overruling old habits of pushing too hard, demanding too much, or getting too caught up in accomplishing some small piece of work does, in fact, put us back into the state of mind that is psi-conducive: slowing down, seeing the larger picture, connecting with the whole, and experiencing the abundant nature of time, space, and one another.

22. PRACTICE FORGIVENESS

Letting go of old resentments that keep the heart tight and closed is also part of opening to psi. A lot of energy can otherwise get blocked, trapped, and diverted into the full-time job and hard work of maintaining anger and resentment. And as I've said repeatedly, opening up our intuitive channels is about *having a lot of focused, coherent energy.*

It happens that practicing meditation, operating with kindness, and leaning into feelings of compassion, love, and gratitude will make the practice of forgiveness almost easy, at least for extended periods of time. In fact, many aspects of this process of psi enhancement are likely to increase your capacity for forgiveness. Watching your ego with a smile will also take you a long way.

Of course, practicing forgiveness is not the same as continually exposing ourselves to people and situations that are harmful to us. Forgiveness doesn't mean being dumb and going back for more abuse; it's about letting go and moving on. Harboring resentment is a needlessly expensive way to remind ourselves to keep out of harm's way. We can just avoid the harm and save ourselves the energy.

I like what Sonia Choquette says when she talks about forgiveness as a struggle for the ego but not for the soul. She says, "The ego, ruler of the ordinary, is a very fragile and brooding entity. It doesn't like to be hurt or humiliated. The soul, however, doesn't like to cling to the past. . . . [It knows that] all experiences ultimately teach us something. . . . When we can find the lesson, we can be free of the experience and the pain. The soul knows that no one else can control it." Forgiveness is a natural by-product of remembering who we really are.

23. AMPLIFY FEELINGS OF LOVE AND GRATITUDE

Of all the emotions in the whole human spectrum, love and gratitude are the ones most capable of catapulting us out of earthbound clock time and into the space-time that is the territory of psi.

Vivian Bochenek says that love—the big, transpersonal kind—is what creates the miracles in her physician's office. Valerie Hunt talks about a generalized feeling of lovingness, which is felt all over the body, not just in the heart, and produces a "vibration of coherency." Judith Orloff talks about how, when she feels an emotional connection to someone she is tuning in to, she gains access to tremendous amounts of psi information. Itzhak Bentov says that love is the basis for the very force of gravity—that we all hold together on this planet for love.

Rosalyn Bruyere talks about how love is an emotion that essentially allows for *expansion*—that when she opens her heart, her whole field *swells* and she can pull in more energy, hold more energy, and generate more energy for her healing work.

In fact, she feels that it is only by opening up her heart that she can both run energy through her body and perceive psychically at the same time. "Love gives me the power to run both systems at once," she says, adding, "I have an obligation to love at the beginning of each healing; and at the end, I am grateful for having had the opportunity to love."

So the practice is simple: as many times as it occurs to you, and you can genuinely feel it, look at things with love, take them into your heart, and feel gratitude for them. Let things and people touch you, and go ahead and feel them deeply. Love the smell of morning, the kid in the grocery store, the drive to work, or the memory of a sweet time. Obviously, you can't do this all the time, and some days it will be well-nigh impossible. But take these moments for yourself regularly and often.

And the more you can let the emotion of gratitude wash through you, which I like to think of as a kind of *high-test* lovingness, the more you pump up your field and create more coherence for opening to psi. I love Vivian Bochenek's description of driving to work and feeling gratitude and wonder for all the people, all over the world, who made her car for her. This is the openhearted consciousness of a child, pure and present and huge.

These suggestions, in addition to the imagery in chapter 6, are guaranteed to further open your psi capacities. I know the list is a long one, but it's pretty comprehensive and at the same time rather simple. In addition to increasing psi sensitivity, following these suggestions will also likely be good for your physical, emotional, and spiritual well-being, so please give them your serious consideration.

Some General Cautions and Ethical Concerns

It is always a good idea to proceed slowly when developing your psi skills in order to give your physical and emotional systems time to adapt to the changing energy levels you'll be negotiating. Otherwise, certain vulnerable places in the body might bear the brunt of the sudden shifts in energy that take place. Although from our current knowledge it's impossible to claim a direct, causal link, there is some reason to suspect that the temporal lobes of the brain and/or the various glands of the endocrine system can get overloaded and symptomatic from too rapidly developing psi skills.

Of course, the reverse causal relationship might be true, too: endocrine system anomalies and temporal lobe disorders might be what produces psi phenomena in some people. And another

possibility is that they both are part and parcel of the same phenomenon and occur concomitantly without any causal connection.

However, just to be on the safe side, we should consider the
possibility that rapid psychic growth, without certain safeguards, can lead to physical problems for some people. The intuitives in my study reported a higher-than-average incidence
of epilepsy,[1] migraine headaches, and bouts (almost always
temporary) of hyperthyroidism, hypothyroidism, irregular or
interrupted menstrual periods, hyperinsulinism, hypoglycemia, narcolepsy, cystic breasts, kidney stones, and one case
each of Graves' disease, early menopause, and a benign pineal
gland tumor that liked to come and go at odd times.

As I've mentioned earlier, possibly this is because these
glandular systems have the job of *modulating* these energy
shifts. Quite probably this is where the higher frequencies of
pulsing psi data from the field are adapted and transduced into
usable levels for the human body. Otherwise, as Sue Greer explains, it would be a little like trying to run a strong current of
electricity through a weak wire. Things could get a bit fried.[2]

In a similar vein, Joe McMoneagle suggests that the operation of psi might be about the conversion of energy states. Joe,
who has had two full-blown near-death experiences (and several other incidents where he nearly died but without seeing
the tunnel and the white light), has experienced a heart attack,
convulsions, open-heart surgery, hepatitis B, and a helicopter
crash and is highly sensitive to shifts in energy. He gets a sharp
pain in his left eye, like a needle, about twenty-four to forty-
eight hours before a substantial energy shift on the planet, such
as an earthquake, tidal wave, or major hurricane.

In order to receive powerful psi information and avoid having the body take a beating in the process, the receiver's energy
field needs to be pumped up, full and strong. Our energy levels
need to be heightened and expanded first, before we can com-

fortably hold and carry the intense currents of psi information that are pulsing into our physical system.

One way to heighten energy levels is through loving-kindness meditation, which opens the heart and expands the energy field through and around the body, allowing the practitioner to pull in, contain, and use these higher amplitudes and frequencies. The imagery offered to you in chapter 6 is designed to help you do this.

Another way to heighten energy levels is through physical exercise. In fact, it was apparent to me from my sample that the people who were most actively engaged in regular physical activity, especially the body-oriented and/or movement meditation practices,[3] had the fewest problems with physical symptoms. As Emilie Conrad-Da'oud, the developer and a daily practitioner of Continuum, a system of meditative body movements, told me, "The movement balances you so well, you don't drain your organs. Your state expands to accommodate wide fluctuations in energy levels."

So my first caution is to take your time and, if possible, build your skill levels slowly and incrementally so that your body can naturally accommodate the changes; and second, I advise building up your own energy field through loving-kindness meditation and regular physical exercise and movement meditation. As always, balance is the key.

However, it is not just your physical body that needs to accommodate and integrate the energy and information that's coming to you; you need a spiritual and ethical system to hold it as well. Without the grounding container of strongly implanted moral principles, any one of us could abuse this powerful gateway to knowledge. We could say this, of course, about any impressive talent or skill.

I don't want to give the impression that I see ethics as a separate issue here, however. On the contrary, a strong sense of what is right seems to develop quite integrally as part of becoming skilled and familiar with opening to psi in a thoughtful way, and most of the people I spoke with ended up with similar "rules and regs" for themselves, even though they arrived at them independently of one another.

In Joe McMoneagle's words, as ability grows and psi experiences accrue, "you're restructuring your beliefs, your ideas about reality, and you can't help but gain a fuller, more complex understanding about what constitutes what is right. You go beyond temporal constructs to something much more stringent than man's law. You transcend localized rules to a more holistic understanding of the human race." Most of the people in my study held themselves to a higher standard than the prevailing norms and were much stricter with themselves, more scrupulous about their daily behavior.

Gregory Kehn puts it in a more personal way: "You can't separate the way you live your life from this practice." He feels it is not enough for him to be pure and clear during the times he is sitting with a client; he feels bound to push for greater purity and clarity in every part of his life, on or off duty. Nor is it sufficient, he says, merely to gain access to accurate information; the information should serve a higher purpose and be accompanied by continual spiritual guidance.

Bryan Christopher, too, talks about the need for leading a life that reflects the consciousness of what he is trying to teach. He watches his thoughts and judgments from moment to moment so he can keep his heart open, not just in a reading, which is pretty effortless for him, but in the grocery store or airport, which is more difficult.

Decisions about what to do with the information you receive are sometimes hard to make—what to tell someone, what to keep to yourself; how to phrase something in the most helpful way, how to decide what is none of your business. Psychiatrist, author, and clairvoyant Judith Orloff, M.D., suggests that it is committed spiritual practice that gives her the necessary tools to help her make these decisions well.

Some also feel they are helped by the ethical constraints of their professions. Several psychotherapists suggested that responsibly using intuitive information wasn't much different from just being a responsible, professional psychologist, doctor, pastor, social worker, or counselor. And, in fact, the code of ethics published by the Academy of Psychic Arts and Sciences (found in appendix C) does indeed look much like any professional counselor's code.

I'll be discussing these broader ethical guidelines based on the thinking and experiences of the people I spoke with as well as on what I've derived through my own experience.

IF THEY DON'T ASK, YOU DON'T OFFER

Given the unbound, free-floating nature of psi, it is essential that we be extra-respectful of people's boundaries and sense of privacy. This means keeping out when we haven't been invited in. If someone doesn't ask for information, the general rule of thumb is to keep quiet—a rule, I might add, that applies to the more mundane kinds of advice giving as well.

Maine intuitive Winter Robinson says, "I never work without agreement." And, as one woman put it, "You don't turn on the equipment without permission"—no looking into people's lives out of simple curiosity or self-interest. And for those who, like Bryan Christopher or Iris Saltzman, have equipment that never really turns off and whose choices are to either "engage or stay in neutral," the choice is to stay in neutral unless given permission and asked otherwise.

Judith Orloff tells of a painful lesson she learned early in her career, when she told a pregnant woman that her unborn child would have a serious learning disability. The woman became extremely angry and upset. Even though years later the information turned out to be correct, there was nothing the mother could do about it at the time,[4] and Judith regretted telling her so early. Now, she says, "I assess carefully whether or not to say something. I never blurt things out, and I never say anything just to be right."

Several of the people in my study commented on how, when they were in social gatherings, people would frequently ask them, either coyly or nervously, whether they were reading their minds. One intuitive rolled his eyes and told me, "The last thing I want to be doing at a party is checking out what's going on in someone else's head! I don't get to spend enough time in my own head." This sentiment was echoed by several people. Not only was this kind of voyeuristic mind-hopping not experienced as a temptation for these seasoned professionals, but the idea was downright wearisome—a busman's holiday for a hardworking intuitive.

Usually the question that follows this dictum about respecting privacy is, "What about the times you get information that has dire consequences for the person if it's ignored? Don't you have an obligation to butt in and tell them?" Joe McMoneagle says if he gets information about someone's health and it's information that wasn't requested of him, he won't interfere. He says, with typical matter-of-fact sincerity and without a trace of callousness, "It's none of my business. I have no right to interfere with their process. Let it unfold the way it was meant to. It's their adventure, not mine."

Similarly, Miami intuitive and teacher Iris Saltzman, when asked the same question, said she usually doesn't tell people when she sees they are going to die. "Let it be a happy surprise," she says.

As you can see, what may be dire to many of us isn't dire to these spiritually based practitioners. Trekking around and exploring beyond space-time offers a very different take on reality, and "dire consequences" become interesting adventures (usually with lessons attached to them) and happy surprises.

When I asked Bryan Christopher, "What do you do when you see something really horrific happening?" he got his puzzled look and then answered, "I don't see it that way. I don't think anything that happens can be horrific—it's just part of the journey."

Cynthia Gale cautions that sometimes, even when people ask for information, it's not always a good idea to give it to them. She told me, "People can be limited when they're told what's likely to happen. When I get information, I get really quiet, and I ask if there's anything I'm supposed to do with it. Sometimes there isn't."

Greg Kehn reminds us that, regardless, "We can't force a change in someone else's life" anyway, because this "goes against natural law." Iris Saltzman says she never tells people what to do, just offers enough information for them to make informed choices of their own. And Emilie Conrad-Da'oud says, in her typically sensible, balanced way, "I won't say anything negative. Who am I, anyway?"

A couple of people mentioned that sometimes when they get information they work with it in other dimensions, respecting the rules of privacy of this dimension. So Mary Sherman might have her spiritual guides arrange a tête-à-tête with the guides of the other person and let them work it out in dream time. There is a certain integrity and balance to this approach, where the information that is received in the altered state gets examined and used there as well.

Ken Cohen operates similarly when the people involved aren't capable of speaking for themselves, either because they have Alzheimer's or are in a coma or may be a very young child. In these cases, he asks his own sources of spiritual guidance to help him choose the right and proper action. Jim Kepner, too, says, "You don't do things that are going to affect someone else without their permission. If that's not possible, then check with your or their guidance."

DO NO HARM

Another very basic rule of thumb: do not use psi information to harm, disempower, disable, or manipulate anyone at any

time. Don't use it to show off, work your own agenda, cultivate dependency, or feed your appetite for power, money,
love, or friendship. The information should be offered only to
uplift, empower, and clarify options, always with respect for
the other person's freedom and right to choose for himself or
herself.

Emilie Conrad-Da'oud says, "I try to never give anyone anything but encouragement. Maybe I'll warn them if I see they're
getting drained, but that's something they can do something
about."

Similarly, Kathlyn Rhea will tell people about illnesses or
deaths only if she perceives that the information is useful and
can help them with making more informed choices. "I might
tell someone about an upcoming illness—the whys of it and
how to go about correcting it. And once, when someone's dad
was going to die, I mentioned it so the whole family could go
home and make amends with one another. It was a powerful
healing for everyone, and it probably wouldn't have happened
if they'd thought they had more time."

Similarly, Christine Page, when she gets information about
someone's illness, always frames it as a choice: "I always tell
them, well, you could do this and this, or you could do this and
this." Sue Greer also tries to give people information they can
work with themselves. She says, "It's like picking up a thread
that's been dropped and handing it back to someone, so they
can have personal responsibility for it once more."

Mary Jo McCabe describes her typical approach when a
client is asking her how she can help her difficult, abusive husband change his ways. Rather than answering the question directly, she might respond with, "Look, you've seen he's not
about to change, at least not right away. He's had a hard time
with his feelings for a very long time. So *you* need to decide
whether or not you want to stay with him the way he is." This is
very similar to the approach a therapist might take.

Marcia Emery says she always tries to put information in a growth context, to help people discover their own options. She also likes to phrase things in such a way that she's not coming across as the font of all wisdom and the bearer of absolute, immutable truth. Instead, she'll say, "I have a hunch . . ." or "I had a dream . . . ," which she feels gives people more freedom to take or leave what she has to offer. Vivian Bochenek, too, likes to phrase things as her perception rather than as *The Truth*.

One way or another, the people I interviewed made it a practice of looking to their own inner voice or spiritual guidance, so they could discern what was in a person's highest interest to know and how it should be said.

KEEP IT CONFIDENTIAL

Another important rule of thumb: keep all the information confidential. This means many things: not discussing people's lives with anyone else outside of a session or a consultation; not revealing specific information about a third party to the person in the room, except in a circumspect, disguised way, if it will help someone protect himself or herself; and avoiding disclosures of any kind if there is reason to feel uncomfortable about the motivation of the person seeking the data.

As Kathlyn Rhea advises, "You don't talk about people you serve, in the same way that a chaplain or a doctor or a therapist wouldn't. I don't see that there's any difference—it's the same kind of obligation."

For some people, confidentiality never becomes an issue. Bryan Christopher, for instance, can never remember what he's told people shortly after their readings, so being a blabbermouth really isn't an option for him. This was true for several of the people I spoke with. (This probably has something to do with spending a lot of waking, functioning time in theta and delta states.)

Medical intuitive and physician Mona Lisa Schulz, who gives health readings over the phone, will not discuss anyone other than the person she is speaking with directly and will not read for anyone who hasn't personally asked her to. Karyn Greenstreet feels the same way. She will tell people enough to help them protect themselves from someone else but no more, and the focus of the information is always on the people she is speaking to and *their* choices, not on those of the third party.

Sometimes people show up as messengers for someone else. In that case, homeopathic physician Christine Page advises, "You can help them without specifically spilling the beans." She gave as an example a time when a young woman whose boyfriend was dying of AIDS came to see her. The psi data that she got was that the boyfriend would be dying soon, that he in fact wanted to die and was tired of fighting his illness, but that his girlfriend (the messenger) was having a hard time letting go of him. At some level, Christine felt this young man was asking that Christine help his girlfriend pull back so he could move on. Christine was moved to encourage the girlfriend to start attending to her own needs and taking better care of herself and, by focusing her in this way, fulfilled what she felt was needed by both of them without violating her code.

Like Christine Page, Greg Kehn feels that frequently people come in as messengers for another. "If a person is there as a catalyst for helping someone else, spirit will go ahead and give me the information; they [the guides] shut down or tell me 'none of your business' when the person's motives are manipulative." When he senses that people are just being nosy about other people, he simply tells them "I'm not picking anything up."

Similarly, Joe McMoneagle always demurs from disclosing information when he is not in agreement with a person or an assignment. "I wouldn't challenge anyone directly," he said. "I'd just say I wasn't getting anything." Victor R. Beasley, too, always asks his own guidance if it is appropriate for someone to have the information they are seeking.

Another related caution: it's usually a good idea in social situations to keep your own counsel when you hear about something happening that you had already foreseen through precognition. Although it's a natural, human impulse to exclaim, "Hey, I knew that!" there's usually no benefit to doing so, and you run the risk of setting up a power dynamic between you and your friends that interferes with your relationships.

Problems can arise if friends are constantly being reminded of your psychic skills: it sets you apart from them, it creates a one-up situation, and it encourages dependency on you. And you can also wind up feeling exploited: people might start restricting their contact with you to times when they feel they need information from you.

OTHER CAUTIONS AND MISCELLANEOUS ADVICE

To recap other concerns mentioned throughout this book: don't get caught up in rooting for certain outcomes in the information you are seeking; if you can't stand away from your judgments and personal investments, your information is likely to be tainted.

Also, always try to be cognizant of the ways that you are likely to distort, project, and muddy up the data. Most people are more likely to be wrong in some areas than in others. "Know when your own personal filters get activated," says Karyn Greenstreet, "because, believe me, they will be."

Because of this, you don't want to set yourself up as the font of all wisdom and healing for others. It is far wiser and fairer to know that you will be wrong from time to time and never to promise people otherwise. Whenever possible, it's good to encourage people to use other sources of information as a check on what you are offering them—most importantly, their own instincts, good sense, and intuition. The intuitives in my study used everything from physicians' diagnoses to police and army intelligence reports to astrological charts as external sources of information to counterbalance and validate their own.

Because it is imperative never to use your psi skills to show off, manipulate, weaken, or disempower others or to feed your need for power, respect, friendship, intimacy, or money, this requires being especially vigilant at times of loneliness or neediness in your life, when, as a teacher or advisor, it would be ever so easy to slip into an exploitative relationship with a student or a client and find convenient ways to justify it.

Some people felt it was important to do a certain proportion of pro bono work. Iris Saltzman, for instance, hosts a clinic two evenings a week for people who cannot afford her regular fees. And Ken Cohen, trained in various Native American healing practices, will take no money, only gifts, for his individual healing work. This is in keeping with his training.

And one final point: know when to close down shop, too. Take a break, go shopping, read some trash, laugh with your friends, play some killer tennis, sing along with some really *loud* rock 'n' roll on your car radio, or in some other way indulge in a little earnest shallowness now and then. Sooner or later, even transcendent, insightful, and spiritual practice can get a little— forgive the pun—*old*. So keep your balance. Take the time to cut yourself some slack and get silly.

Brief Bios of the Intuitives[1]

Victor R. Beasley, Ph.D., is a consultant to corporations, small businesses, and individuals. His special focus is on intuitive skills training, vision-driven decision making, organizational troubleshooting, team building, conflict resolution, and personal coaching. He has written *Intuition by Design* (Livermore, CA: Oughten House Publications, 1995) and can be reached at 15443 N. 19th Way, Phoenix, AZ 85022. Phone 602–971–5956; fax 602–971–7376.

Vivian Bochenek, R.N., D.O., is an osteopathic physician with a large family practice in Cleveland, Ohio. She offers structured training programs in energy medicine and hands-on healing. Send inquiries to 5592 Broadview Rd., Suite #106, Parma, OH 44134.

Rev. Rosalyn Bruyere is the founder and director of the Healing Light Center Church in Sierra Madre, California. She is also a nationally known teacher and trainer of hands-on healing, clairvoyance, and energy medicine, and the author of

Wheels of Light: Chakras, Auras and the Healing Energy of the Body (New York: Fireside, 1994). Send inquiries for the Rev. Bruyere to the Healing Light Center Church, 261 E. Alegria Ave. #12, Sierra Madre, CA 91024. Phone 818–306–2170; fax 818–355–0996.

Johanna Caroll is a spiritual advisor in San Diego, California, where she consults with individuals and also offers corporate seminars and presentations on "Spiritual Quality Management" and "The Intuitive Bottom Line." She has produced a tape series called *In Search of Spirit* and a workbook by the same name. Send inquiries to P.O. Box 325, Carlsbad, CA 92008. Phone 619–942–8966.

Laura Chapman, M.A., has a counseling and energy healing practice in Cleveland, Ohio. She also offers structured training programs in intuitive development and healing, where she combines traditional and nontraditional methods. She can be reached at 2026 Murray Hill Road, #207, Cleveland, OH 44106. Phone 216–229–4111.

Bryan Christopher offers psychic consultation by telephone to individuals, couples, and groups and is the founder and director of the Foundation in Light, where he also offers a retreat experience and meditation tapes. He can be reached at 3 Abanico Road, Santa Fe, NM 87505–8396. Phone 505–466–6314.

Judith Lee Cohen, R.N., M.Th., is both a nurse and a massotherapist who works clairvoyantly and teaches workshops in energy healing and integrative body therapy around the country. She is currently practicing and teaching in Tucson and can be reached by writing 6411 North Treasure Drive, Tucson, AZ 85704–5613. Phone 520–297–2968.

Kenneth S. Cohen, M.A., M.S.Th., is a healer, teacher, and writer who has in-depth knowledge of chi kung and tai chi chuan as well as many Native American healing traditions. His book *The Way of Qigong: The Art and Science of Chinese Energy Healing* is scheduled for publication by Ballantine in spring of 1997. Sounds True of Boulder, Colorado (800–333–9185), has produced several of his audiotapes, including *Chi Kung Meditations, Taoist Healing Imagery,* and *The Way of Chi Kung.* Send workshop inquiries to P.O. Box 234, Nederland, CO 80466.

Emilie Conrad-Da'oud is a teacher and trainer and the founder and director of the organization Continuum, named for a method that combines movement, breath, and sound to produce profound growth, insight, healing, and change. Inquiries can be sent to 1629 18th Street #7, Santa Monica, CA 90404. Phone 310–453–4402; fax 310–453–8775; e-mail Continuummove@earthlink.net.

David Davis, Ph.D., is an intuitive trainer, corporate consultant, and individual counselor in Reston, Virginia. He has in-depth knowledge of energy and healing, which he integrates successfully into his corporate work. Send inquiries to him at 489 B Carlisle Drive, Herndon, VA 22170. Phone 703–478–2729.

Marcia Emery, Ph.D., is a psychologist, consultant, lecturer, and author who specializes in teaching people how to cultivate their intuition. She has written *Dr. Marcia Emery's Intuition Workbook* (Englewood Cliffs, NJ: Prentice-Hall, 1994) and has produced an audiotape set entitled *Intuition: How to Use Your Gut Instinct for Greater Personal Power* (Nightingale-Conant, 1995). You can reach her by writing to 1502 Tenth Street, Berkeley, CA 94710. Phone 510–526–5510; fax 510–526–9555.

Brian Fleisher is the founder and director of EnergyWorks, where he functions as a healer, teacher, and trainer. He is a certified Barbara Brennan practitioner and focuses on spiritual and energy healing, and integrating body and spirit. Send inquiries to 725 N. A1A, C–207, Jupiter, FL 33477. Phone 407–575–3530.

Cynthia Gale is a fiber artist, lecturer, and clairvoyant reader. She provides workshops and retreats on Mother Earth Spirituality and helps people design their own personal ceremonies, using the ritual objects that they create with her from feathers, bone, leather, and stone. She also provides psychic information to help people with their lives, either on the phone or in her Earth Prayers Gallery at 2078 Murray Hill Road, Cleveland, OH 44106. Phone 216–231–0103.

Karyn Greenstreet is a multitalented professional psychic, intuition development instructor, and spiritual counselor. She owns and operates NorthLight, where she holds classes in psychic development and provides individual psychic readings. Inquiries can be mailed to NorthLight, P.O. Box 1406, Morrisville, PA 19067. Phone 215–295–3132; e-mail karyn@cis.compuserve. com.

Rev. Sue Greer is a clairvoyant reader, energy healer, and teacher. She does psychic readings, intuitive medical diagnosis, and physical/spiritual healing at her Rising Phoenix Healing Center. She also offers a two-year apprenticeship program for healers that begins each fall. You can write to the center at 1323 Apple Ave., Silver Spring, MD 20910. Phone 301–589–9349.

Valerie Hunt, R.P.T., Ed.D., is a researcher, innovator, author, and international lecturer who studies the human vibratory field and builds lab equipment to measure it. She has written *Infinite Mind: The Science of Human Vibrations* (Malibu, CA: Malibu Publishing, 1995) and has also published several lecture, meditation, and auric sound tapes, available on video and/or audio. Direct inquiries to Malibu Publishing Co., P.O. Box 4234, Malibu, CA 90265. Phone 310–457–4694; fax 310–457–2717.

Rev. Gregory Kehn is a medium, teacher, lecturer, and counselor and a lifetime member of the Lily Dale Assembly in upstate New York. Nationally known for his detailed and precise psychic abilities, he is regularly consulted by police departments, attorneys, and health professionals. His busy practice usually means a wait of several weeks or even months for an appointment. Inquiries should be sent to 663 Hazel St., Girard, OH 44420. Phone 216–545–2062.

Jim Kepner, Ph.D, is a psychologist and senior faculty member at Cleveland's Gestalt Institute. He has a busy practice in body-oriented psychotherapy and teaches energy healing classes and workshops on intuition. He has written *Body Process* (San Francisco: Jossey-Bass, 1992) and *Healing Tasks* (San Francisco: Jossey-Bass, 1995). Inquiries can be sent to 20600 Chagrin Blvd. #750, Shaker Heights, OH 44122.

Rev. Kenneth Koles, Ph.D., has a holistic health practice, teaches tai chi chu'an, and gives workshops on natural healing and energy medicine. His degree is in holistic health sciences and psychology, and he integrates intuitive information with his knowledge base. Send inquiries to him at 2224 Grandview Ave., Cleveland Heights, OH 44106. Phone 216–721–4950.

Mary Jo McCabe is an intuitive counselor, teacher, and author who operates her busy practice out of the McCabe Institute in Baton Rouge, Louisiana, where she provides workshops, readings, and consultations. She has written *Learn to See* (Grass Valley, CA: Blue Dolphin Publishing, 1994) and provides taped readings over the telephone. (There is a wait for appointments.) You can reach the Institute at 9151 Interline, #2B, Baton Rouge, LA 70809. Phone 504–926–3355; fax 504–924–3451.

Joe McMoneagle, CW2, USA, Retired, continues to participate in remote viewing experiments, both as a paranormal subject and as a science associate, through his company Intuitive Intelligence Applications, Inc. He describes his experiences in his book *MindTrek: Exploring Consciousness, Time and Space Through Remote Viewing* (Charlottesville, VA: Hampton Roads, 1993; phone 800–766–8009). You can contact him by mail at P.O. Box 100, Nellysford, VA 22958. E-mail: mceagle@comet.net.

Jane Miller, M.S.W., applies her intuitive skills to her lesbian/gay psychotherapy practice in Cleveland and Oberlin, Ohio, where she takes a holistic approach to healing and growth. You can reach her at 12417 Cedar Road, #21–24, Cleveland, OH 44106. Phone 800–457–0345.

Caroline Myss, Ph.D., is an internationally known medical intuitive, author, and lecturer who now spends much of her time offering workshops and training (she no longer does individual consultations). Her latest audiotape is *Energy Anatomy*

(Boulder, CO: Sounds True, 1996), and her new book is called *Anatomy of the Spirit* (New York: Crown, 1996). Please send inquiries to Self-Health Systems, Brindabella Farms, 5607 S. 222nd Rd., Fair Grove, MO 65648.

Judith Orloff, M.D., is a psychiatrist, clairvoyant, and author. She describes her experiences in her book *Second Sight* (New York: Warner, 1996). She can be reached by writing 2080 Century Park East, Suite 1811, Los Angeles, CA 90067. Phone 310–277–7007.

Christine Page, M.D., is a British homeopathic physician, author, lecturer, and intuitive counselor who holds seminars on intuitive development, mind/body medicine, and energy healing. She has authored *Frontiers of Health* (Saffron Walden, England: C. W. Daniel, 1992) and *The Mirror of Existence* (Saffron Walden, England: C. W. Daniel, 1995). Send inquiries to her at 36, Warwick Road, Beaconsfield, Bucks, HP9 2PE, England.

Helen Palmer is a well-known intuitive, lecturer, and author who gives workshops throughout the U.S. and Europe. She has an audiotape, *Intuition Training* (Boston: Shambhala, 1993), and a six-tape set on *The Enneagram* (Boulder, CO: Sounds True Audio, 1995). She has written three books on the Enneagram, the latest two being *The Enneagram in Love and Work* (San Francisco: HarperSanFrancisco, 1995) and *The Pocket Enneagram* (San Francisco: HarperSanFrancisco, 1995).

Terrye Powell is a psychic reader from Scottsdale, Arizona. You can write her for more information at 9275 East Mission Lane #202, Scottsdale, AZ 85258.

Lee Pulos, Ph.D., is a corporate trainer, seminar leader, sports psychologist, writer, and entrepreneur. Send inquiries to him at 1260 Hornby Street, Second Floor, Vancouver, British Columbia, V6Z 1W2, Canada. Phone 604–669–6979.

Kathlyn Rhea is an intuitive counselor, teacher, and author who consults widely with law enforcement agencies (including the FBI, the Secret Service, Scotland Yard, and many U.S. police and sheriff departments). She is the author of *The Psychic Is*

You (Berkeley: Celestial Arts, 1979) and *Mind Sense* (Berkeley: Celestial Arts, 1988) and frequently appears on national television. Send inquiries to her at 34 Carnoustie Drive, Novato, CA 94949. Phone/fax 415–884–2120.

Lynn Robinson, M.Ed., is a psychic reader, teacher, and trainer, well known in the Boston area. Her individual consultations are both spiritually and psychologically oriented. Her sessions are also available by phone. For more information, write her at 53 Langley Road, Suite 260A, Newton Center, MA 02159. Phone 617–964–0075.

Winter Robinson, M.Ed, M.A., is an intuitive reader, author, teacher, and lecturer who leads seminars on psychic development, intuitive diagnosis, and creativity. She has written *Intuitions: Seeing with the Heart* and *Remembering: A Gentle Reminder of Who You Are* (both from Buxton, ME: Tor Down, 1995) and an audiotape, *Discovering Intuition* (Buxton, ME: Tor Down, 1993, 1995). Send inquiries to 430 Simpson Road, Saco, ME 04072. Phone 207–929–6960; fax 207–929–6901; e-mail Winter@mixnet.commedesign.com.

Deborah Rozman, Ph.D., a psychologist, is the executive director of the Institute of HeartMath and the author of *Meditating with Children* (Boulder Creek, CA: Planetary Publications, 1993). Send inquiries to the Institute of HeartMath, P.O. Box 66, 14700 West Park Avenue, Boulder Creek, CA 95006. Phone 800–372–3100.

Kevin Ryerson is an internationally known intuitive reader, lecturer, consultant, and author who was first brought to national prominence by actress Shirley MacLaine's enthusiasm for his work. He offers phone consultations, workshops, and seminars and can be reached by writing P.O. Box 151080, San Rafael, CA 94915. Phone 415–454–9727; fax 415–454–9865.

Iris Saltzman is a well-known medical intuitive and psychic reader who provides private consultations in the Miami area and by phone. She is the founder of the International Parapsychology School, where she consults, provides readings, holds seminars, and offers free clinic evenings for the indigent. Her work was nationally spotlighted by a very impressed Brian Weiss, M.D., in his book *Many Lives, Many Masters*. Send inquiries to the school's director, Beverly Penzell, at 1893 N.E. 164th St., N. Miami Beach, FL 33162. Phone 305–944–2781; e-mail: ipps@mcimail.com.

Marilyn Schlitz, Ph.D., is the director of research for the Institute for Noetic Sciences, and for years has been a parapsychology subject, researcher, and investigator in various remote viewing experiments. She can be reached at IONS at 475 Five Gate Rd., #300, Sausalito CA 94965. Phone 415–331–5650; e-mail mschlitz@well.sf.ca.us.

Mona Lisa Schulz, M.D., Ph.D., is a medical intuitive who also happens to have a Ph.D. in neuroanatomy and training in neuropsychiatry. She provides readings over the phone, describing a person's health in the context of his or her emotional life. She is also a popular presenter and is currently working on her first book. She can be reached at P.O. Box 452, Yarmouth, ME 04096. Phone/fax 207–781–8973.

Mary Sherman, M.A., is a counselor and clairvoyant in the Cleveland area who is frequently consulted both personally and professionally for her intuitive insights. Send inquiries to her at 2043 Campus Road, South Euclid, OH 44121.

Don Treadwell is the director of the Center for Spiritual Growth in Dana, Indiana, where he provides personal consultations and intuitive training programs. Send inquiries to P.O. Box 714, Dana, IN 47847. Phone 317–665–3665.

Alan Vaughan, Ph.D., is an intuitive consultant, trainer, researcher, and lecturer, as well as Adjunct Professor of Intuitive Studies at Atlantic University in Virginia Beach, Virginia. He has written *The Power of Positive Prophecy* (London: Harper-Collins, 1991) and *Psychic Reward: Intuition-Training Software* for either IBM or Mac users. Send inquiries to 1567 Silverwood Drive #B, Los Angeles, CA 90041. Phone 213–255–8256; fax 213–257–4242; e-mail AlanPsy@aol.com.

Rhea White, M.L.S., is a parapsychology researcher who directs the Exceptional Human Experience Network and edits *The Exceptional Human Experience Journal,* along with a newsletter, *EHE News.* She collects and documents experiences of a psychic, mystical, peak, or synchronistic nature. She has written *In the Zone: Transcendent Experience in Sports* with Michael Murphy (New York: Penguin, 1995). Send requests for information to her at The EHE Network, 414 Rockledge Road, New Bern, NC 28562. Phone 919–636–8734; fax 919–636–8371; e-mail 76460.633@compuserve.com; Web site: http:// www4. coastalnet.com/ehenet

The Questionnaire

I asked the following questions of the intuitives I interviewed:

Subject name:
Address:
Phone:
Referred by:
General History:

If not mentioned spontaneously in the history, I asked about these characteristics:[1]

bilateral dominance
dyslexia
seizures
migraines
motion sickness
effects on watches, lightbulbs, appliances
history of trauma or abuse
near-death experiences

UFO sightings or encounters
training in dance, music, theater, art, etc.
endocrine anomalies
sleep disturbances
sibling position

Psi Q and A

1. What do you call this ability? How do you perceive it?
2. What are some examples of it?
3. What is your experience of receiving it? How does your body feel? Are your senses involved? If so, which ones? If not, how does it come to you?
4. Where do you think this information comes from?
5. Have you always been able to do this? Or was there a specific time or a general time in your life when it started?
6. If you experienced this ability as a child, how was it handled in your family or by others around you when you were growing up?
7. Were there certain times when the information seemed to come to you more than others? Or times when it became dulled or unavailable to you?
8. Are there areas where you know your information is more reliable than others? Or less? Any consistent blind spots?
9. How do you know when you're off, or do you?
10. Do you have ethical rules to guide you with this? If so, what are they?
11. Do you engage in any purposeful practice to cultivate this ability? Or is there anything in your life that just naturally cultivates this?
12. Are there times when it seems to go away? Can you identify what is operating when this happens?
13. Is there something specifically about you that you connect or attribute this ability to?
14. What else do you consider yourself really good at?
15. How would you describe yourself, your personality, your way of being in the world?
16. Does this ability seem to run in your family?
17. Anything else I should know? What didn't I ask you that I should have?

Code of Ethics of the Academy of Psychic Arts and Sciences[1]

We protect the sanctity of client relationships and information.

We maintain a safe, sensitive and supportive environment to facilitate personal growth and enrichment for all.

We value our client's time as our own.

We enforce the universal gift and responsibility of free-will choice.

We describe our services and products truthfully and without exaggeration. We highlight that we have no supernatural powers, cannot cause nor prevent any occurrence.

We explain that results from our work vary by individual.

We are forthright about the terms and conditions under which we work.

We communicate immediately any fee we charge for products or services. We base our fees on time or costs involved, never escalating solely for agency of need nor client emotional state.

We suggest alternatives to those in financial hardship.

We avoid divided loyalties, hidden agendas and dual relationships which could compromise our judgment.

We guard against creating unhealthy dependency or abiding disrespect for the profession.

We better the profession as a whole by keeping current with developments, furthering our education and experience, sharing our results and research and acting as mentors to those less experienced.

While we absolutely reserve our right to choose for whom we work on the basis of individual consideration, we pledge to honor and maintain the academy's more than 20 years' tradition for ethical and social responsibility by making our services and products available without regard to gender, race, national origin, marital status, sexual orientation, social standing, advanced age or physical status.

Notes

Preface

1. Just a cautionary note: This was very individualized imagery for this particular woman and not a general recipe for guided imagery for multiple myeloma.

Introduction

1. I provide a more detailed description of the research in chapters 1 and 2 of my book *Staying Well with Guided Imagery,* where I describe these and other studies supporting these claims.
2. See Richard Broughton, *Parapsychology: The Controversial Science* (New York: Ballantine Books, 1991), 134.
3. Extra thanks to Jeffrey Mishlove, Ph.D., director of the Intuition Network; Marilyn Schlitz, Ph.D., research director for the Institute of Noetic Sciences; Ruth Buczynski, Ph.D., president of the National Institute for the Clinical Application of Behavioral Medicine; and Anne Simpkinson, editor of *Common Boundary* magazine, for their time, opinions, and recommendations.

Chapter 1: Clarifying Some Terms

1. More specifically, the *clairs* get broken out into subcategories of clairvoyance, clairaudience, and clairsentience to differentiate among information that is picked up through the senses of seeing, hearing, and feeling.

2. Herbert Simon, a professor of psychology and computer science at Carnegie-Mellon University, makes use of chunk concepts and discusses them in "Making Management Decisions: The Role of Intuition and Emotion" in *Academy of Management Executive* (February 1987).

3. This, by the way, is a standard technique for checking oneself for accuracy—"erasing" the image and then seeing if it persists. I learned it from Anne Armstrong, one of the earliest intuitive trainers with a solid, national reputation.

4. This description is from Philip Goldberg's *The Intuitive Edge* (Los Angeles: Jeremy Tarcher, 1983), 46.

Chapter 2: How People Come to Be Psychic

1. And actually, some of these factors may not be psi-conducive at all but rather psi-responsive instead. Endocrine symptoms, for instance, may occur as the result of the physical body's attempts to accommodate the wide energy shifts that happen when psi ability is expanding rapidly. And some of these other traits may simply be concomitant factors—artistic ability and psi may be different aspects of the same thing, for instance. So we mustn't assume a simple cause-and-effect relationship here.

2. Reported in Russell Targ and Keith Harary, *The Mind Race* (New York: Ballantine Books, 1984).

3. The most statistically significant finding I came up with in my small sample was a significantly greater amount of bilateralness in the people who had the most psi skills (chi-square $(1,41) = 6.74$, $p = .009$).

4. Michael Grosso calls attention to the importance of family and community norms supporting the development of psi in his

discussion of the early lives of Padre Pio, Sathya Sai Baba, and Jesus in *Frontiers of the Soul* (Wheaton, IL: Quest Books, 1992).

5. Joe describes this in greater detail in his book *Mind Trek* (Charlottesville, VA: Hampton Roads, 1993).

6. Bruce Greyson, "Increase in Psychic Phenomena Following Near-Death Experiences," *Theta* 11 (1983): 26–29; Richard Kohr, "Near-Death Experiences, Altered States and Psi Sensitivity," *Anabiosis* 3 (1983): 157–76; Kenneth Ring, *Heading Toward Omega* (New York: William Morrow, 1984); Cherie Sutherland, "Psychic Phenomena Following Near-Death Experiences," *Journal of Near-Death Studies* 8 (1990): 93–102.

7. All six of the people who had had full-blown NDEs felt certain that the experience had increased their psychic ability; and almost half of my sample (eighteen) had had partial NDEs.

8. Neuropsychologist Michael Persinger discusses this in his article "Modern Neuroscience and Near-Death Experiences," in *Journal of Near-Death Studies* 7 (1990): 233–39, and in "The 'Visitor' Experience and the Personality: The Temporal Lobe Factor," in *Cyberbiological Studies of the Imaginal Component in the UFO Contact Experience,* ed. D. Stillings (St. Paul, MN: Archaeus Project, 1989): 157–71.

9. Michael Persinger, "The Tectonic Strain Theory as an Explanation for UFO Phenomena: A Non-Technical Review of the Research, 1970–1990," *Journal of UFO Studies* 2 (1990): 105–37.

10. See Paul Devereux's book *Earth Lights Revelation* (London: Blandford, 1989).

11. Kenneth Ring, Ph.D., a professor at the University of Connecticut, is widely known and respected for his research on near-death experiences. His book, *The Omega Project: Near-Death Experiences, UFO Encounters, and Mind at Large* (New York: William Morrow, 1992), spells out these ideas.

12. Jenny Randles's study is discussed in her book *Abduction* (London: Robert Hale, 1988).

13. Although this may sound alarming, we have these tiny seizures all the time during sleep.

14. In my sample, 14.6 percent reported a history of seizures, and 17.1 percent experienced migraine headaches.

15. Biofeedback uses electronic equipment to measure subtle changes in the body, such as brain waves or galvanic skin response, by way of sensors attached to the scalp or fingertips. The machine then signals the information with a sound tone, light, or picture on a screen. With this kind of instantaneous feedback about their physiological processes, people are able to consciously control supposedly autonomic functions, such as blood pressure and brain waves.

16. There are four major types of brain wave patterns: beta, alpha, theta, and delta. We now have far more sophisticated ways to measure these things, but the Greens set up the distinctions among them in this way: *Beta* waves in the brain (13 to 26 Hz, or cycles per second, and higher) are associated with active attention, usually focused on the outer world and including concrete thought. Reading a book or watching a baseball game takes place primarily with beta waves. *Delta* rhythms (0.5 to 4 Hz) are found in people who are sleeping or unconscious. *Theta* waves (4 to 8 Hz) are associated with near-unconscious or subliminally conscious states. They appear as a person becomes drowsy and starts falling asleep and are associated with any deep quieting of the body, emotions, and thoughts. Hypnagogic images appear in this state and can take the form of a crystal-clear sensory memory, a creative insight, or a sudden pop of ESP. *Alpha* rhythms (8 to 13 Hz) accompany a state of relaxation with awareness—a more aware state than theta. Closing the eyes produces brief bursts of alpha, as does focusing on a daydream or interior image, even if the eyes are open. If someone's eyes become glazed while you are speaking to them, they are probably in alpha, and, as you know, not paying attention to you.

17. See Rollin McCraty, William A. Tiller, and Mike Atkinson, "Head-Heart Entrainment: A Preliminary Survey" (Boulder Creek, CA: Institute of HeartMath, n.d.).

18. Charles Honorton, "Psi and Internal Attention States," in B. B.

Wolman, ed., *Handbook of Parapsychology* (Jefferson, NC: McFarland, 1986), 453–72.

19. *Entrainment* is the inherent tendency of vibrating particles to want to vibrate in sync with one another. The pendulums of several clocks left in the same room will sooner or later start to ticktock together, with the weaker oscillations making the necessary adjustments to match the stronger ones. So, too, people's vibrational fields will tend to synchronize, the weaker signals becoming entrained to the rhythms of the stronger ones.

20. Interestingly enough, drug experimentation was not frequently mentioned by my interviewees as a catalyst for psi opening. Most of the people I spoke with did not use drugs, and several had gone to some trouble to steer clear of them. However, a few people did say that LSD, peyote, and other substances had given them a preview of the expanded perceptions they would later experience.

21. Stephen Levine's grief meditation in his book *Healing into Life and Death* (New York: Doubleday, 1987) is an excellent example. I'm partial to the imagery exercise from my *Health Journeys* series audiotape, *For People Experiencing Grief* (Los Angeles: Time-Warner AudioBooks, 1993).

22. There's a wonderful description of these events in Patricia Love's *Hot Monogamy: An Audio Seminar on the Essential Steps to More Passionate, Intimate Lovemaking* (Boulder, CO: True Audio, 1994).

23. Certainly one doesn't need to be a care giver to experience working in this way; any kind of behavior, done consciously and with an open heart, will do.

Chapter 3: Setting the Stage

1. See pages 76–77 and 80–84 for a summary of the research of Kenneth Batchelder, Charles Honorton and Russell Targ, and Hal Puthoff.

2. Except for a very small minority; Vivian Bochenek, Kevin Ryerson, and a couple of others reported that being tired actually improved certain of their abilities.

3. Disciplines that teach meditation practice usually caution the meditator against becoming caught up in the excitement of these psychic pops and allowing psi phenomena to distract from the process of spiritual growth. For this reason, they usually advise ignoring them.

4. Guides were variously described as the spirits of healers and spiritual teachers no longer among the living (referred to by one man as "very smart dead people"), different aspects of the higher self, power animals, angels, and nonhuman or alien guides.

5. She learned this way of tuning in to psi from a method called *integrated awareness* developed by a Chicago psychic named Connie Newton, who now lives outside of Atlanta, Georgia.

6. For excellent, clear directions on how to teach yourself to see auras, check out Barbara Brennan's instructions in her book *Hands of Light* (New York: Bantam Books, 1988).

7. The original sheep-goat studies can be found in Gertrude R. Schmeidler and Robert A. McConnell, *ESP and Personality Patterns* (1958; reprint, Westport, CT: Greenwood Press, 1973). You can find a recent summary by John Palmer entitled "Extrasensory Perception: Research Findings," in *Extrasensory Perception*, ed. Stanley Krippner, *Advances in Parapsychological Research*, vol. 2 (New York: Plenum, 1978): 59–243.

8. K. J. Batcheldor, "Report on a Case of Table Levitation and Associated Phenomena," *Journal of the Society for Psychical Research* 43 (1966): 339–56. And Kenneth J. Batcheldor, "Contributions to the Theory of PK Induction from Sitter-Group Work," *Journal of the American Society for Psychical Research* 78 (1984): 105–22.

9. C. Brookes-Smith and D. W. Hunt, "Some Experiments in Psychokinesis," *Journal of the Society for Psychical Research* 45 (1970): 265–81; and C. Brookes-Smith, "Data-tape Recorded Experimental PK Phenomena," *Journal of the Society for Psychical Research* 47 (1973): 69–89.

10. From Iris M. Owen and Margaret Sparrow, *Conjuring Up Philip* (New York: Harper & Row, 1976).

11. Anne can be heard working in her unique way on a series of tapes from a workshop she and Jim gave at Esalen Institute. It is called *Psychic/Intuitive Training, A Weekend Workshop on Tape, with Anne and Jim Armstrong* (Pine Grove, CA: Azoth Institute, 1987).

12. Victor R. Beasley, Ph.D., *Intuition by Design* (Livermore, CA: Oughten House Publishers, 1995).

13. Richard S. Broughton, Ph.D., *Parapsychology, The Controversial Science* (New York: Ballantine, 1991), 132–37.

14. This can be found in Michael Grosso's book *Frontiers of the Soul* (Wheaton, IL: Quest Books, 1992).

15. Thirty-eight out of forty-two people said they needed regular doses of time spent in nature.

16. R. McCraty, W. Tiller, and M. Atkinson, "Head-Heart Entrainment: A Preliminary Survey" (Boulder Creek, CA: the Institute of HeartMath).

Chapter 4: Letting It Happen

1. Unfortunately, the term *channeling* now refers almost exclusively to a process of making way for various spirit "entities" to take over the body and voice of a host—in other words, old-time Spiritualist psychism. I prefer to use the term for the more general phenomenon of allowing energy, great ideas, intuitive hunches, and inspiration to move through us, *while we remain in possession of our bodies and our personalities.*

2. See D. Patrick Miller's interview of Helen Palmer in *Intuition,* no. 7. *Intuition* magazine is available from Intuition, P.O. Box 460773, San Francisco, CA 94146.

3. A nice summary of this important but still undervalued work can be found in Irvin L. Child's "Psychology and Anomalous Observations: The Question of ESP in Dreams," *American Psychologist* 40 (1985): 1219–30. The original work is a little harder to get hold of: *Dream Telepathy: Experiments in Nocturnal ESP,* 2d ed. (Jefferson, NC: McFarland, 1989).

4. Honorton extended the idea that interior focus would increase psi with his *ganzfeld* studies. His experiments tried to replicate the inward focus of sleep in awake subjects by creating an artificially homogeneous sensory field. Halved Ping-Pong balls were placed over the subject's eyes, with diffuse, red light showing through them to reduce visual input to a uniform pink glow; unpatterned white noise was sent through earphones to reduce auditory input; and the subject lay in a comfortable reclining chair to reduce and stabilize tactile input. Subjects thus were cut off from outside distraction while remaining in a waking state.

   So outfitted, subjects were asked to report their spontaneous images while someone in the room next door focused on a randomly chosen picture. These tests and the many experiments that followed established the ganzfeld as a highly repeatable way of liberating psi, and reassured Honorton of the soundness of his thinking. Marilyn Schlitz of the Institute of Noetic Sciences has since replicated and reexamined several ganzfeld studies. We can assume that psi will indeed thrive nicely with interior focus and in the absence of competing external stimuli. Honorton, "Psi and Internal Attention States: Information Retrieval in the Ganzfeld," in Betty Shapin and Lisette Coly, eds., *Psi and States of Awareness* (New York: Parapsychology Foundation, 1978), 79–90.

5. From Ingo Swan, *Natural ESP, A Layman's Guide to Unlocking the Extra Sensory Power of Your Mind* (New York: Bantam Books, 1987), 33.

6. This actually occurred in the Targ/Puthoff study and is described in Russell Targ and Keith Harary, *The Mind Race* (New York: Ballantine Books, 1984).

7. From her set of eight tapes, *Psychic/Intuitive Training: A Weekend Workshop on Tape,* by Anne and Jim Armstrong (Pine Grove, CA: Azoth Institute, 1987).

8. In fact, traditional acupuncture points are found at key junctures and crossroads in these lines.

9. This has to do with the surplus of negative ions that exist in ocean air, running water, and night air in general. They like to attach to

the positive ions in our field, and in so doing, expand it. For a more thorough discussion of heightening energy, read Richard Moss's *How Shall I Live* (Berkeley, CA: Celestial Arts, 1985).

10. Researchers Elmer and Alyce Green established the truth of this principle in their book *Beyond Biofeedback* (New York: Delacorte Press, 1977).

11. An astonishing 73.2 percent of my sample reported dramatic periods of electrical disturbances with appliances and/or magnetic disturbances with watches. Some people told me they couldn't wear anything but a very expensive quartz watch; others could keep only the humble Timex running on their wrists.

12. Well-known author and near-death experience researcher Kenneth Ring discusses these phenomena in his book *The Omega Project* (New York: William Morrow, 1992); see chapters 5 and 9 of that book. According to Dr. Ring, people who report UFO incidents have a high incidence of both ESP and this blitzing effect on appliances.

13. Even now, at a very vibrant age eighty, she is still getting new grants, zealously building new equipment, and expanding her field of inquiry. But as early as the 1970s, she was using a copper room and measuring the energy generated by the shifting moods, ideas, and imagery of her two subjects, Rosalyn Bruyere and Emilie Conrad-Da'oud, both exceptionally endowed healers and teachers with ample energy fields. You can read about her work in her book *Infinite Mind: The Science of Human Vibrations* (Malibu, CA: Malibu Press, 1995).

Much later, Elmer Green at the Menninger Foundation did a similar study of eight gifted psychic healers. (Again Bruyere was one of them, and Ken Cohen as well. Bruyere, Conrad-Da'oud, and Cohen were all interviewed for my study.)

And now, both the Fetzer Institute and the Institute of Noetic Sciences are sponsoring several ongoing studies that look either directly or obliquely into these energetic phenomena, particularly as manifested in distant healing, intentionality, biofields, and subtle energy effects.

14. By hearing about other people's descriptions of their experience, we're better able to perceive our own. So, at the risk of overkill, here are a few more:

   Rosalyn Bruyere describes energy as a tingling around her eyes and forehead, along with sensations of tingling down the back of her neck. Sometimes this is accompanied by a feeling of the bones of her head shifting—a subtle but palpable movement of the plates of her skull and in the musculature around her cranium.

   Dr. Christine Page, a homeopathic physician and holistic healer from the United Kingdom, feels a kind of pressure and tingling on the back of her head and in the center of her forehead, "as if someone were putting a hand on it," along with a warm pressure around the heart.

   Gregory Kehn describes this same heightened experience of energy waves moving through his body.

   Bryan Christopher described an initial feeling of the back part of his head starting to grow big and heavy. He also feels a kind of "power surge" that changes his very metabolism. When I asked him if this felt uncomfortable, he looked at me oddly, paused, and finally said that it had nothing to do with either comfort or discomfort. Clearly, his experience of energy expansion in his head went so far beyond the world of physical sensation that my question seemed to actually disorient him for a moment.

   Similarly, Cynthia Gale reported that as she began to move into her "seeing" mode, "My body feels lighter. I'm less aware of the burden of my physical body."

15. Keep in mind that both sound and color are forms of vibration, have their own frequencies and amplitudes, and thus, in a very elemental way, fit the definition of energy.

16. Having observed Bryan Christopher both before and immediately after he has given a one-hour session, I can attest to the visible, metabolic changes in him. His upper body becomes flushed and swollen—so much so that he usually has to unbutton his cuffs and loosen his shirt collar. His face and neck also

become several shades pinker. Johanna Caroll has also observed that her clothes usually feel tight after a reading and that sometimes a certain amount of belt loosening is in order. Healer Rosalyn Bruyere agrees that there is a metabolic component to all this energy shifting, and medical intuitives Iris Saltzman and Sue Greer also feel certain that the endocrine system is heavily involved in this process.

17. And, as you will see in the next chapter, all experience is basically about energy.

Chapter 5: Explaining It

1. Thanks for this chapter go to Fred Alan Wolf, who was very generous with his time and ideas, and whose book *The Dreaming Universe: A Mind-Expanding Journey into the Realm Where Psyche and Physics Meet* (New York: Simon & Schuster, 1995) was a great help; to Norman Friedman for writing *Bridging Mind and Spirit: Common Elements in David Bohm's Physics, the Perennial Philosophy and Seth* (St. Louis, MO: Living Lake Books, 1994); to Valerie Hunt for *Infinite Mind: The Science of Human Vibrations* (Malibu, CA: Malibu Publishing, 1995), and finally to my hero, the awesome Itzhak Bentov, author of *Stalking the Wild Pendulum: On the Mechanics of Consciousness* (Rochester, VT: Destiny Books, 1988).

2. The dramatic exception here is Freud's brilliant and quickly disaffected student Carl Jung, who took a much broader view of human nature and explored spirituality and common cross-cultural human thematic principles, called *archetypes,* in great depth. His work was seen as interesting but useless until fairly recently. It is only now, as we are approaching the close of the twentieth century, that there is a wide resurgence of interest in his work.

3. There are interesting echoes here of "In the beginning, when God began to create heaven and earth—the earth being unformed and void."

4. The simplest, clearest description of this process that I have ever found, comprehensible even to the severely physics-challenged, is in Itzhak Bentov's brilliant classic, *Stalking the Wild Pendulum*.

5. From the James Gleick book *Chaos: Making A New Science* (New York: Viking Penguin, 1987).

6. One cycle per second is called a *Hertz* in technical language.

7. This could be why so many people find they have greater psychic ability after they receive a severe electrical shock. According to intuition trainer Lee Pulos, severe shock produces a *biasing* effect that makes the person's energy more coherent.

8. The Institute for Heart Math (IHM) can be reached at P.O. Box 66, Boulder Creek, CA 95006; phone 800-372-3100; e-mail: hrtmath@netcom.com.

9. Doc Lew Childre, *Cut-Thru* (Boulder Creek, CA: Planetary Publications, 1995), 75–76.

10. McCraty's frequency numbers are much lower than the range first offered by Elmer and Alyce Green in the 1970s, when their biofeedback experiments defined alpha, beta, delta, and theta states. According to the Greens' system, a frequency of .1 could only mean deep sleep. This apparent discrepancy, according to McCraty, is caused by the far greater sophistication in equipment that is now available to measure the lower frequencies. Better instrumentation and amplification tools result in our seeing the spectrum of human brain waves as ranging from roughly 0–40 Hz.

11. See R. McCraty, W. Tiller, and M. Atkinson, *Head-Heart Entrainment: A Preliminary Survey* (Boulder Creek, CA: Institute of HeartMath, n.d.); the publication is available from the Institute of HeartMath, Research Division, Electrophysiology Lab, 14700 West Park Avenue, Boulder Creek, CA 95006. See also William A. Tiller, Ph.D., Rollin McCraty, M.A., and Mike Atkinson, "Cardiac Coherence: A New, Noninvasive Measure of Autonomic Nervous System Order," *Alternative Therapies* 2, no. 1 (January 1996): 52–65.

12. Bentov, *Stalking the Wild Pendulum*, 122.

13. Bentov, *Stalking the Wild Pendulum,* 122.

14. Fred Alan Wolf is author of *The Dreaming Universe* (New York: Simon & Schuster, 1994) and *Parallel Universes* (New York: Simon & Schuster, 1988) and is a nationally known synthesizer of consciousness research and modern physics.

Chapter 6: Imagery to Access Psi

1. This group synergy phenomenon is true for any guided imagery endeavor and is perhaps most dramatically found in patient support groups that employ imagery to combat cancer, diabetes, and the like. Even people who find it virtually impossible to make any headway with the technique by themselves can have a powerful experience in a group. And once having gained access to psi in the group, they can then go home and manage it on their own, as if the route had been mapped in the mind and now can be taken again.

2. Take a look at *Staying Well With Guided Imagery* (New York: Warner Books, 1994) for a more elaborate explanation of how touch is probably the most powerful adjunct to imagery we can employ.

3. Strong feelings of fear simply cannot coexist with strong feelings of love and gratitude. Focus strongly enough on generating loving feelings, and the fear will abate.

4. Without this instruction, certain people will spend the entire time searching for the exact best place to go to. They never get to experience the exercise.

5. The beginning part of this imagery is very similar to the imagery I used in many of the beginning imagery segments of my *Health Journeys* tape series (New York: Time-Warner AudioBooks, 1992–1994) and several of the imagery scripts in *Staying Well With Guided Imagery* (New York: Warner Books, 1994).

6. The beginning, heart-expanding part of this imagery is a variation on my "Imagery for Healthy Boundaries," which can be found in *Staying Well With Guided Imagery* (New York: Warner

Books, 1994); and on Tape One, Side B of my *Health Journeys* audiotape *For People Experiencing Stress* (New York: Time-Warner AudioBooks, 1993).

7. The beginning part of this imagery exercise is taken from "Imagery to Re-inhabit the Body" in *Staying Well with Guided Imagery* (New York: Warner Books, 1994), 79–82.

8. Parts of this imagery were taken from *Staying Well With Guided Imagery,* "Transforming a Symbolic Issue on a Screen" (New York: Warner Books, 1994).

9. The essence of this exercise can be found in *Staying Well With Guided Imagery* (New York: Warner Books, 1994) and on the *Health Journeys* audiotape, *For People Working on Their Relationship* (New York: Time-Warner AudioBooks, 1993).

10. Taken from the *Health Journeys* tape *For People Working on Their Relationship* (New York: Time-Warner, 1993).

Chapter 7
Specific Things You Can Do to Cultivate and Maintain Psi

1. See the resource section at the back of this book for specific workbooks and training programs.

2. In Sonia Choquette's *The Psychic Pathway* (New York: Crown Trade Paperbacks, 1995): 27–29.

3. I've recorded a walking meditation that's especially good for fidgeters. It's the last exercise on *Health Journeys* audiotape *For People Experiencing Stress* (New York: Time-Warner AudioBooks, 1995).

4. For more information, contact Continuum, 1629 18th Street #7, Santa Monica, CA 90404. Phone 310–453–4402; fax 310–453–8775; e-mail Continuummove@earthlink.net.

5. I think this is true for many people but definitely not for everyone. Some people are more cognitively organized, and they become more and more sensitive to ideas about things and not so much to feelings as they open up psychically.

6. Kathlyn Rhea, *Mind Sense* (Berkeley: Celestial Arts, 1988).

Chapter 8: Some General Cautions and Ethical Concerns

1. The causal relationship with epilepsy could be the other way around: epilepsy could produce highly intuitive states. Some studies show marked similarities between the experience of temporal lobe seizures and intuitive states, including the time of day in which they occur. Both seem sensitive to low electromagnetic energy frequencies.

2. Dr. Vivian Bochenek suggests that possibly those who regularly struggle with energy depletion might be trying to do more psychically than their physical systems can handle at the time. She treats many energy healers in her practice and sees a lot of "blown-out endocrine systems, hypoglycemia, candida, chronic fatigue, and depression." She feels this happens when people are pushing too hard and not tempering their psychic growth with a concern for balancing their physical systems.

3. This would include chi kung, tai chi, yoga, and the Continuum practices.

4. The child was in fact diagnosed as hyperactive and is now on Ritalin for his condition. It is quite possible that the diagnosis was made early because the mother was on the lookout for it due to Judith's intervention. However, Judith feels that the information was given to the mother so early that it caused her several years of needless upset.

Appendix A: Brief Bios of the Intuitives

1. Except, of course, those who preferred to remain anonymous.

Appendix B: The Questionnaire

1. These factors were mentioned so frequently by my subjects that I eventually went back and requestioned all the respondents about them and incorporated them into the questionnaire.

Appendix C: Code of Ethics of the Academy of Psychic Arts and Sciences

1. Courtesy of Timothy Lattus, Director, Academy of Psychic Arts and Sciences, Dallas, TX .

Resources

Books

Barbara Ann Brennan. *Hands of Light: A Guide to Healing through the Human Energy Field.* New York: Bantam, 1987.

Itzhak Bentov. *Stalking the Wild Pendulum: On the Mechanics of Consciousness.* Rochester, VT: Destiny Books, 1988.

Richard S. Broughton. *Parapsychology: The Controversial Science.* New York: Ballantine Books, 1991.

Sonia Choquette. *The Psychic Pathway: A Workbook for Reawakening the Voice of Your Soul.* New York: Crown Trade Paperbacks, 1994.

Larry Dossey. *Healing Words: The Power of Prayer and the Practice of Medicine.* San Francisco: HarperSanFrancisco, 1993.

Norman Friedman. *Bridging Science and Spirit: Common Elements in David Bohm's Physics, The Perennial Philosophy, and Seth.* St. Louis, MO: Living Lake Books, 1994.

Philip Goldberg. *The Intuitive Edge: Understanding Intuition and Applying It in Everyday Life.* Los Angeles: Jeremy Tarcher, 1983.

Michael Grosso. *The Frontiers of the Soul: Exploring Psychic Evolution.* Wheaton, IL: Quest Books, 1992.

Valerie V. Hunt. *Infinite Mind: The Science of Human Vibrations.* Malibu, CA: Malibu Press, 1995.

Mary Jo McCabe. *Learn to See: An Approach to Your Inner Voice through Symbols.* Nevada City, CA: Blue Dolphin, 1994.

Jeffrey Mishlove. *The Roots of Consciousness: The Classic Encyclopedia of Consciousness Studies.* Tulsa, OK: Council Oak Books, 1993.

Belleruth Naparstek. *Staying Well with Guided Imagery: How to Harness the Power of Your Imagination for Health and Healing.* New York: Warner Books, 1994.

Kenneth Ring. *The Omega Project: Near-Death Experiences, UFO Encounters, and Mind at Large.* New York: William Morrow, 1992.

Jane Roberts. *The Nature of Personal Reality.* New York: Bantam, 1980.

Ingo Swann. *Natural ESP: A Layman's Guide to Unlocking the Extra Sensory Power of Your Mind.* New York: Bantam, 1987.

Russell Targ and Keith Harary. *The Mind Race: Understanding and Using Psychic Abilities.* New York: Ballantine Books, 1984.

Frances E. Vaughan. *Awakening Intuition.* New York: Anchor Books, 1979.

Fred Alan Wolf. *The Dreaming Universe: A Mind-Expanding Journey into the Realm Where Psyche and Physics Meet.* New York: Simon & Schuster, 1994.

Audiotapes and Videotapes

Caroline M. Myss and C. Norman Shealy. *Vision, Creativity & Intuition.* Phone/fax: 417–467–3102. Video.

Belleruth Naparstek. *Health Journeys: For People Working on Their Relationship* (1994); *For General Wellness* (1994); *For People Experiencing Stress* (1995). New York: Time-Warner AudioBooks. Audio.

Helen Palmer. *Intuition Training.* Boston: Shambhala Lion Editions, 1993. Audio.

Winter Robinson. *Discovering Intuition.* Buxton, ME: Tor Down, 1995. Audio.

Workshops and Training Programs

Continuum (Emilie Conrad-Da'oud), 1629 18th Street #7, Santa Monica, CA 90404. Phone 310–453–4402; fax 310–453–8775; e-mail Continuummove@earthlink.net.

Discoveries of the Intuitive Heart (Henry Reed, Ph.D.), 503 Lake Drive, Virginia Beach, VA 23451. Phone 804–422–0371.

Earth Prayers Gallery (Cynthia Gale), 2078 Murray Hill Road, Cleveland, OH 44106. Phone 216–231–0103.

EnergyWorks (Brian Fleisher), 961 N A1A #128, Jupiter, FL 33477. Phone 407–575–3530.

Foundation in Light (Bryan Christopher), 3 Ababico Road, Santa Fe, NM 87505–8396. Phone 505–466–6313.

Healing Light Center Church (Rosalyn Bruyere), 261 E. Alegria #12, Sierra Madre, CA 91024. Phone 818–306–2170.

McCabe Institute (Mary Jo McCabe), 9159 Interline #3B, Baton Rouge, LA 70809. Phone 504–926–3355.

Northlight (Karyn Greenstreet), P.O. Box 1406, Morrisville, PA 19067. Phone 215–295–3132.

Rising Phoenix Healing Center (Sue Greer), 1323 Apple Avenue, Silver Spring, MD 20910. Phone 301–589–9349.

School for Spiritual Healing and Prophecy (Greg Kehn), P.O. Box 252, Lily Dale, New York 14752. Phone 716–595–2159.

Self-Health Systems (Caroline Myss, Ph.D., and Norm Shealy, Ph.D., M.D.), Brindabella Farms, 5607 South 222nd Road, Fair Grove, MO 65648.

GUIDED IMAGERY AUDIOTAPES
BY BELLERUTH NAPARSTEK

Health Journeys for specific health problems:
  For People with Asthma
  For People with Cancer
  For People with Diabetes
  For People with Headaches
  For People with High Blood Pressure/Heart Disease
  For People with HIV Infection
  For People with Multiple Sclerosis
  For People with Rheumatoid Arthritis/Lupus
  For People with Stroke

The Health Journeys Recovery Series:
  A Meditation to Help You Recover from Alcohol and
    Other Drugs
  A Meditation to Help You Stop Smoking
  A Meditation to Help You with Weight Loss

Health Journeys for general physical and emotional health:
  For People with Depression
  For People Experiencing Stress
  For People Experiencing Grief
  For Anyone Concerned with General Wellness
  For People Coping with Pain
  For People Working on Their Relationships

Health Journeys for medical procedures:
  For People Undergoing Chemotherapy
  For People Undergoing Surgery

For inquiries about Belleruth Naparstek's speaking schedule,
or for questions, feedback, requests for new tapes or to receive
Health Journeys Network News, please write to Image Paths,
Inc., at 2635 Payne Avenue, Cleveland, Ohio 44114, call 800-
800-8661, or e-mail hjtapes@aol.com.